THEY GAVE ALL FOR FREEDOM

The powerful true story of one family's quest for freedom, and the two countries they served.

Susan Trout Armstrong

Vlasta Honolka

John Honolka in Prague before WWII: John is wearing the coat he later wore to prison. Valuables hidden in the coat's lining—money, jewels, and chocolate bars—helped the family to escape.

First published by Armstrong Bookplate, 2026
www.armstrongbookplate.com

Second edition

ISBN: 979-8-234-02937-9

Printed in the United States of America

Cover art, caged bird illustration, and book design by
AC Strategic Marketing, Kristen Nuss and Miho Halsey

Dedicated To

The children of war,
and all who knock at freedom's door

In Memory Of

John & Jarmila Honolka
the parents who gave up everything for their family's freedom
&
Eva Honolka Newman
the daughter who kept their dream alive

The caged bird sings

with a fearful trill

of things unknown

but longed for still

and his tune is heard

on the distant hill

for the caged bird

sings of freedom.

—Maya Angelou, *The Caged Bird*

"I've found that there is always some beauty left

—in nature, sunshine, freedom, in yourself; these can all help you."

—Anne Frank, *The Diary of a Young Girl*

PREFACE

This story whispered to me long before I knew of the Czechoslovakian Honolka family or met their youngest daughter. It began when, as a teenager, I read *The Diary of Anne Frank*; and my heart wept for the children lost through war.

Decades later, before I connected with Vlasta Honolka, I walked the town square of Prague and marveled at the ancient astronomical clock—a beloved landmark in her homeland. I visited the site of a WWII prison in Hungary and strolled the narrow cobblestone streets of Vienna—unaware that I followed in the shadow of the family's own footsteps, during their imprisonment in Budapest and the long journey to Displaced Person's Camps in Austria and Germany.

Closer to home, the summer before Vlasta phoned me, my husband and I traveled to the Amana Colonies of Iowa on a road trip, driving through the gentle hills from one tiny town to the next. We felt the sunshine, breathed in the fresh air, and admired the historic building that once housed a baked goods factory—the same factory John Honolka managed in his adopted country.

As karma would have it, while I unknowingly explored the locations of her childhood, Vlasta searched for a writer to tell the family's story. She noticed an ad about an author in her local newspaper, clipped it out, and tucked it into a drawer. Retrieving it two years later, she dialed my number.

In our first conversation, Vlasta and I spoke about synchronicity: the coincidences that led her to me, and those that connected me to her family's journey. This is why I have no doubt the story deserves to be told, and it is why I am grateful to be her storyteller. I write it with deep appreciation to my friend, Vlasta Honolka, the little sister who never gave up on publishing the story. And with love to my Bruce, always.

TABLE OF CONTENTS

CHAPTER ONE

JARMILA

Czechoslovakia, 1920

If she had known all the tragedy she would endure in her lifetime, baby Jarmila might have fought, kicking and screaming, to be born somewhere else. Somewhere far from the politics of Czechoslovakia.

But then, her firstborn daughter might never have received the Cross of Merit from the Czech Minister of Defense, or the prestigious Americanism Medal from the Daughters of the American Revolution in the U.S.

Their story begins in a country smaller than the state of New York, but far older, in a part of Europe that was first settled by the Celtic, then Germanic, and finally Slavic tribes over a period of several hundred years. It wasn't until 1918 that the modern country of Czechoslovakia was born. It was shortly after WWI, and the United States of America played an important role in the process.

Czech politician and philosopher Tomáš Garrigue Masaryk, a political emigrant visiting the U.S., used his connections to argue for the dissolution of Austria-Hungary and the creation of a new national state of Czechs and Slovaks. Masaryk connected his hopes with America because of personal reasons. He was married to an American citizen, Charlotte Garrigue, who had traveled to the U.S. a few times before the war and had lectured at the University of Chicago. In October 1918, Masaryk published the Declaration of Czechoslovak Independence, and personally handed it to President Woodrow Wilson, in Washington, D.C. His networking was successful.

Later that month, the Czechoslovak National Committee in Prague proclaimed the independence of Czechoslovakia. On November 14, 1918, while Masaryk was still in the United States, the committee elected him as the first president of the state. He arrived in Prague in December. The following spring, in May of 1919, a plane crash killed two of the country's top leaders—Prime Minister Karel Kramar and War Minister Milan Stefanik. This left President Masaryk and Foreign Minister Edvard Beneš to handle foreign relations, while the leaders of five major parties controlled domestic matters.[i]

When baby Jarmila Kralikova arrived on July 6, 1920, she would spend her lifetime trying to navigate the political turmoil of her country. It would require tremendous strength and stamina even her parents couldn't imagine. Yet, somehow, they prepared her for the challenges ahead.

Jarmila was a darling baby, with bright blue eyes and blonde curls. The youngest of five children born to Marie and Rudolph Kralik, she was adored by her parents as well as her older siblings. Everyone loved Jarmila. She was a calm infant, with a sunny disposition. Perhaps it was because her parents were older when they welcomed her into the world. Her mother, Marie (Roubicek) Kralik, was 39, and her father Rudolph, 41, when Jarmila was born. By all accounts, she was a perfect baby. Even as a toddler, Jarmila was everything they hoped for in a child. She loved to learn new things and was eager to help others.

The little girl loved to play with dolls. At Christmas each year, she dreamed of a new doll with a baby buggy, and her parents complied. They repaired and repainted the previous year's buggy and updated her doll with a fresh wig and clothing.

Both beautiful and engaging, Jarmila was intelligent and inquisitive beyond her years. Her parents treated her like a princess, introducing her to the finer things in life. By the time she was in grade school, little Jarmila already enjoyed symphony concerts and visiting art museums. She was well behaved and clearly comfortable surrounded by adults. She loved to laugh, and her sense of humor delighted those around her.

A city girl, she learned all the skills that were expected of a child in her circumstances. She was taught to knit, crochet, and embroider. Jarmila also loved to swim and soon excelled at diving. She played the violin, and, above all, she enjoyed reading and art.

Jarmila adored her father, who was kind and generous to everyone. He took her to the pastry shop in town as a treat. She sat beside him on the trip, pointing at everything they passed along the way. By age 10, Jarmila had grown used to hearing the political discussions of the adults in her life.

The Great Depression reached Czechoslovakia soon after 1930. Jarmila listened as the adults around her exchanged news about politics and the economy. They read newspaper accounts that the highly industrialized German-speaking districts were hit more severely than the rest of the country. The Germans complained that the Prague government was offering the Czech areas a disproportionate amount of unemployment relief.

Jarmila's father sensed the unrest throughout Czechoslovakia. Adolph Hitler had risen to power in Germany, and the discontent contributed to the rise of militant German nationalism in Czechoslovakia. Each year, the country's tenuous borders seemed more likely to fall apart.

In October 1933, the fall after Jarmila turned 13, the situation worsened. Konrad Henlein, a furtive supporter of Hitler, launched his Sudeten German Home Front.[ii] Professing loyalty to the democratic system, he called for recognition of the German minority as an autonomous body. It was a cause he would champion for the next two years, as the country tried desperately to hold the borders established in 1919.

Although the older generation embraced Jarmila when she was small, those her own age refused to befriend her. Jarmila was too petite. Too pretty. Too admired. Young Jarmila led a solitary life. Determined to make her own mark on the world, she devoted herself to her hobbies. She practiced her diving incessantly, to the point of rupturing her eardrums at the age of 14.

If Jarmila wished for friends her own age, she never complained to her teachers or her family. Instead, she seemed content to be alone and would crawl into the attic in the cold weather to read all winter long. She particularly liked Anna Karenina—drawn to the complexity of historic novels. Just six days before Jarmila's sixteenth birthday, in a storm of publicity, Margaret Mitchell's epic *Gone with the Wind* was released; the young girl couldn't wait to get her own copy. It quickly became a favorite she read again, and again.

In her teen years, Jarmila embraced fashion and hoped to become a milliner. She devoted hours to handcrafting elaborate hats. The solitary pursuit suited her. During a time when others her age were making new friends and socializing, Jarmila retreated further into herself. She dreamed of owning a shop of her own. When Marie Kralikova realized how serious her daughter was about this newest hobby, she put her foot down.

"Get this hat-designing idea out of your head." Marie wagged her finger at Jarmila.

"But, Mother, it is what I want to do," Jarmila said.

"It cannot happen. Millinery is not a decent profession for a young woman. I won't have my daughter demeaning herself."

Though a strong-willed teenager, Jarmila was too respectful to defy her mother's wishes. She became a seamstress instead.

CHAPTER TWO

JARMILA MEETS JOHN

Czechoslovakia, 1935

Perhaps it was inevitable that Jarmila would fall in love with an older man. She had always preferred to converse with adults, after all. She was barely 15 when she first noticed John Honolka at a soccer game.

John was handsome and athletic—a professional football player for the Czechoslovakian Sparta team. He was 25 years old and accustomed to being the star attraction on the field. All the girls sighed when they watched him play. But it was Jarmila who caught his eye. When his teammates had first commented about the beautiful young fan who never missed a game, John had no idea who they were describing. Focused on a game, he rarely looked at the bleachers.

Then, as luck would have it, Rudolph Kralik brought his daughter with him into the village for a shopping trip one Saturday morning, and John walked past them on the sidewalk. Rudolph called out to the athlete.

"Hello, there. Might you be the Spartan football star who helped our team win the game last week?"

John smiled and extended his hand. "I might. Although I'm not sure I scored the winning goal, I do play for the Sparta team." His eyes slid to the girl standing quietly beside her father. "And who is this?"

"Meet my daughter, Jarmila. She's a fan, as well."

John took Jarmila's small hand in his and smiled. "Nice to meet you. Perhaps I'll see you both at the next game."

From that moment forward, John looked for Jarmila at every game. She waited for him outside the gate, where they engaged in animated conversations about sports, school, and the day's events. He admired her quick wit and ready smile; and she adored him for treating her as an equal. Boys her own age had never held her interest the way John did.

It wasn't long before their admiration for each other grew into something deeper. One day, as Jarmila watched John play, she realized she had fallen in love with him the first time he took her hand on the sidewalk. She sat in the middle section of the stadium bleachers, hands clenched, her small body strained toward the goal.

"One more goal, John." Jarmila whispered the request, and the wind carried it to his ear. John Homolka caught the ball in the cradle of his feet, twisted his body into a graceful arc, and kicked it deftly into the corner of the net. The Czechoslovakian football team had won the game.

Jarmila ran to the field and stood on her tiptoes to wrap her arms around John's neck. He leaned down to kiss her check. Despite the difference in their ages, the two were soon inseparable. The petite teenager was head-over-heels in love, and John was eager to make her his bride.

If Jarmila's parents had reservations about their daughter's choice, they didn't voice them. Her father, Rudolph, was a practical man who loved his daughter unconditionally. Her mother, Marie, ruled the household with a strict hand. She had already raised Jarmila's four siblings. Both parents openly acknowledged their youngest daughter as "exceptionally independent." It did not surprise them when their teenager set her sights on the professional soccer player and never looked back.

The same year John and Jarmila fell in love, Czechoslovakia held parliamentary elections; on May 19, 1935, the newly established Sudeten German Party won 44 seats in the Chamber and 23 in the Senate. Funded by the German Nazi Party, it won over two-thirds of the vote amongst Sudeten Germans.[iii] The political climate was changing.

Although the world around them was unsettled, John and Jarmila's devotion to each other remained strong. They married in a small church ceremony, attended by family and friends. The day was fair, with clear skies as blue as Jarmila's eyes as she said her wedding vows. John gazed down at her and pledged to love and cherish his bride until the end of time.

After the service, in a rare moment of warm affection, Marie handed her daughter a beautiful cut-glass bowl. "This was made in Bohemia. My mother gave it to me, and now I pass it on to you. No matter how far away you go, keep it close, and always remember your homeland."

The gift touched Jarmila. She hugged her mother. "I will, Maminko. I promise."

The newlyweds settled in an enchanting mountain region called Krkonose, also known as the Sudetenland by the German population. They made their home in the small town of Trutnov, where Jarmila had lived her entire life. John supplemented his wages from the Sparta team with a career in sales. He went to work first for a local chocolate company, and later a bakery, selling their products to retail shops. Football barely paid the bills of a single man, and he and Jarmila were eager to start a family. Tall and handsome, with a natural gift for sales, John excelled in business.

With friends in many circles, John stayed informed about politics and world affairs. In the fall of 1936, after John and Jarmila married, Adolph Hitler spoke before the German Labor Front introducing his Four-Year Plan to have the German economy ready for war within the next four years. Some saw this as Hitler's continued foreign policy boasting a "natural antagonism" toward the Soviet Union, but others considered Germany's rearmament a direct violation of the strict terms set by the allies of World War I at the Treaty of Versailles.[iv] For John and Jarmila, Hitler's actions were of no concern.

Because Jarmila lived a largely isolated life, she discovered marriage changed everything. Suddenly, she was the center of her husband's world. John's friends and business acquaintances became her friends. She stepped easily into her role as wife and hostess.

Jarmila was an accomplished seamstress, cook, and housekeeper. She welcomed John's guests into their home with gracious hospitality, entertaining them with lively conversations and an occasional violin performance. The popular couple shared many evenings with friends, talking and laughing far into the night. Jarmila had never been happier. The only thing they longed for was a child.

A year after their marriage, the young couple had their wish. Their apartment was next to a military training facility in Trutnov, known in many European nations as Kasarna. The air smelled of early spring and the sunlight gilded the mountain tops with touches of gold. The windows faced a large meadow filled with the blooms of yellow dandelions (Pampelisky) and small white daisies. Here, on May 14, 1937, at five minutes to eight on a Friday morning, on a day filled with sunshine and hope, Jarmila gave birth to their daughter, Eva. A midwife delivered the baby girl. Little Eva weighed just four pounds and was nineteen inches long.

Although John still played soccer part time, he had already become a respected businessman. Now, he was also a father. Having a child of her own thrilled Jarmila. She loved to bathe and feed Eva, and dressed her baby in sweet little hand-sewn outfits she designed herself.

Jarmila's own mother, Grandma Marie, doted on the new addition to the family. On one visit, she wrapped Eva in a soft pink blanket and settled into the rocking chair while Jarmila prepared lunch.

"I always knew you would be a wonderful mother," Marie said to her daughter.

Jarmila smiled. "And why is that?"

"Because you practiced every day as a child."

"Yes. I loved my dolls," Jarmila said.

"You washed their hair till they were bald." Marie chuckled at the memory.

John adored the new baby. When he arrived home from work each evening, he picked up his little girl and crooned to her. Jarmila watched the two of them, her eyes filled with joy. Focused on making a life together with their infant daughter, the two were barely aware of new rumors circulating about a potential German invasion.

John Honolka, in white, was a star football player for the Czechoslovakian Sparta team when he first met Jarmila.

CHAPTER THREE

GERMANY ANNEXES AUSTRIA

Six months later, as Eva cut her first teeth and John's career continued to rise, Adolph Hitler told his military chiefs of his intentions to move against Austria and Czechoslovakia. He planned to embark on an eastward expansion to annex the Sudeten Germans located there. The move was a strategic one, designed to improve the German economy—which had been decimated by the cost of building Hitler's army—and provide a steady food supply.

At the time, Czechoslovakia had the world's seventh-largest economy and was one of the most modern, industrialized countries in Eastern Europe. It was the only nation in Eastern Europe besides the Soviet Union that manufactured its own weapons instead of importing them. Also the world's seventh-largest manufacturer of arms, Czechoslovakia was an important player in the global arms trade, and of particular interest to Hitler.

During a top-secret meeting with his closest confidantes, held at the Reich Chancellery on Nov. 5, 1937, Hitler announced that seizing Czechoslovakia would increase the supply of food under German control, which would lessen the need to import food, thereby freeing up more foreign exchange to import raw materials necessary for the Four-Year Plan's targets. On Nov. 10, 1937, Hitler asked his adjutant, Friedrich Hossbach, to summarize this meeting, which subsequently became known as The Hossbach Conference. Although secrecy shrouded both the Hossbach Memorandum and the meeting, rumors of Hitler's desire to claim sections of Austria and Czechoslovakia spread quickly.[v]

Jarmila was creating a home for her husband and an infant daughter. She

was far too busy to concern herself with politics. The young mother heard
the heated discussions, but she shoved them aside, preferring to spend time
with her baby. She had no way of knowing her idyllic life was about to be
disrupted in ways that would change her forever.

One of the most vocal politicians in the region was Konrad Henlein, now
a leading Sudeten German politician in Czechoslovakia. When he learned
of Hitler's plans, Henlein feared a speedy military defeat for the Czechs.
To avoid the bloodshed—and to assure his own political success—Henlein
offered to help Hitler break up Czechoslovakia from the inside, using
the Sudeten German Party (SdP) to divide the country. He successfully
positioned himself as a free agent representing Czechoslovakia's oppressed
Germans. In reality, his instructions came from Berlin, and his goal was to
give Hitler an opportunity to expand into the country without resorting
to war.

Czechoslovakian politics became more divisive. The political right, led
by the Agrarians, worked to win the support of the Sudeten Germans; the
political left was prepared to cooperate with the Soviet Union. By the spring
of 1938, before Eva had her first birthday, Hitler had accomplished the
"Anschluss" (annexation) of Austria to Germany.[vi]

John and Jarmila listened to a report of the announcement on the
Czechoslovakian shortwave radio station in Prague. It was late Friday
afternoon, March 11, 1938, and Jarmila rocked the baby while John tuned
in the station.

"People are saying the Austrian Chancellor has called for a vote of the
people," John said. "It's to decide whether they want to be annexed by
Germany or remain independent."

"A vote?" Jarmila asked. "Do they truly believe Hitler will allow a vote?"

John shook his head. "It will never happen. Hitler wants Austria, and he
won't stop until he gets it."

Jarmila tucked the blanket more tightly around her sleeping baby before
she turned back to John. "But why Austria?" she asked. "Is it simply because
they speak German?"

"That's what Hitler claims. But others say he wants to control all of Europe."

John adjusted the dial and the news reporter's thready voice filled their living room with the words he always said to open his program. "Hallo. Hallo."

"Events in Austria, of course, occupy the forefront of the pages in Czechoslovakia and elsewhere," The reporter said. "The sudden decision of the Austrian Chancellor, Dr. Kurt von Schuschnigg, to hold a plebiscite at the earliest on Sunday, the 13th of March, for the decision on the independence of the country was judged a surprise to the courts in Vienna."[vii]

He continued in a somber tone, "In the early hours of this morning, reports came from Vienna of demonstrations by the National Socialists in various parts of town."

John groaned and turned the volume lower. "This is what my patriot friends warned would happen," he said to Jarmila. "Hitler will not allow Austria to remain independent."

"Plans for a vote will only enrage him," Jarmila said.

John tuned the volume up again, and the two leaned closer to the radio. The newscast continued:

"And finally, the report that Austria had called up the first tier of the reserve for the preservation of order on the day of the plebiscite. These are matters that naturally rivet the attention of Czechoslovakia," the announcer said.

John stood and paced the floor. "We have reason to be concerned," he said. "We could be next."

Jarmila turned worried eyes to her husband. "If Hitler can annex Austria, there's nothing to prevent him from taking the Sudetenland of Czechoslovakia."

They returned their attention to the program as the announcer confirmed their fears.

"At the same time, reports were forthcoming from Berlin, stating that the sudden decision concerning the plebiscite was disliked in Germany. Today, reports came that Germany has stationed military forces on the Austrian frontier, and that movements of the German army in southern Germany have taken place. Official reports from Berlin revealed surprise at the steps taken by the Austrian chancellor and expressed the expectation that he is aware of the gravity of his actions."

John switched off the radio. "The Chancellor of Austria just made the biggest mistake of his life," he said.

"God help us all," Jarmila said.

Hitler was, indeed, aware of the scheduled plebiscite. He took immediate action—threatening to invade Austria to prevent the vote. When he learned of the coming invasion, Schuschnigg backed down. He canceled the plebiscite and offered to resign to avoid bloodshed.

During a single weekend, Hitler took control. He demanded that the president of Austria, Wilhelm Miklas, appoint an Austrian member of the Nazi Party as the nation's next chancellor. When the president initially refused to do so, Hitler announced an invasion to begin at dawn the next day. Again, the Government of Austria folded under the German ultimatum. In a radio speech to the nation, Prime Minister Schuschnigg declared the dissolution of the Austrian Government and gave authority for running the country to Arthur Seyss-Inquart, the Nazi candidate. Schuschnigg also appealed to the army not to make resistance to the German army crossing the border.

On March 12, 1938, German troops marched into Austria to annex the German-speaking nation for the Third Reich. Enthusiastic crowds met them. Hitler appointed a new Nazi government, and on March 13 the annexation of Austria (the Anschluss) was proclaimed, in a direct violation of the Treaty of Versailles.

On March 15, the Nazis organized several celebrations within the streets of Vienna. Adolf Hitler delivered an impassioned speech from the balcony of HOFBURG, a former Habsburg palace. Hundreds of thousands of Austrians filled the nearby Heldenplatz (Square of Heroes). Hitler declared his plans for the future of the German Reich and Austria—his motherland. The event unleashed a nationalistic frenzy among Czechoslovakia's Sudeten Germans, but it was too late to stem the tide.[viii]

Eva turned one year old in May. To Jarmila, it seemed her baby had barely taken her first steps when, in September 1938, John's prediction came true. Seeking still greater power, Hitler demanded the return of the Sudetenland—a region of Western Czechoslovakia populated largely by German-speaking people—to Germany. He promised his armies would not invade more of Europe if they granted this concession. Now, both Austria and Czechoslovakia were victims of the Third Reich.

The British Prime Minister and French Premier signed the Munich Agreement that September, but Hitler quickly violated the agreement. Suddenly, the Nazis swarmed throughout Czechoslovakia. German-speaking officers filled the shops and streets. Jarmila feared the soldiers who had taken over her city; John vowed to protect his family.

The Germans spread across the country, as their new leader sought to extend his reach into territories he believed should rightfully belong to Germany. The following month, upon the German occupation of Czechoslovakia in October 1938, Konrad Henlein joined the Nazi Party and the SS, the Nazi security forces. They appointed him "Gauleiter of the Sudetenland" and he became responsible for enforcing Nazi Party authority within the area, maintaining the Party's control over the people and life in that region. His betrayal of the Czechoslovakian country was complete.

CHAPTER FOUR

THE WORLD IS CHANGING

1938

If John and Jarmila thought matters could not get worse, they were wrong. Incorporating the Sudetenland into Germany began on Oct. 1,1938. Losing the Sudetenland—the region where extensive Czechoslovakian border fortifications were located—weakened the country's ability to defend itself.

Early in 1939, the British and French governments attempted to help the struggling country. They loaned the Czech government eight million pounds and gifted the country an additional four million. The money was allocated to help resettle Czechs and Slovaks who had fled from territories lost to Germany, Hungary, and Poland in the Munich Agreement and the Vienna Arbitration Award. But their efforts were too late. Within days, the Germans entered the Slovak part of Czechoslovakia, stirring up distrust and leading them to secede from Czechoslovakia. The newly autonomous Slovakia became a puppet of Germany. Still not satisfied with the scope of his regime, Hitler entered Czechoslovakia to "protect them" from the crisis his own Nazis had created.

That spring, Czechoslovakia's northern and southern regions were both under attack. Hungary occupied part of Slovakia. Afraid of an expanding Hungarian invasion, the Czech Prime Minister turned to Germany for protection. Hitler gladly came to the rescue. March 16, 1939, he formed the Protectorate of Bohemia and Moravia, with Baron von Neurath named as Reichsprotektor, an enforcement officer designated to maintain order in the territory. While the negotiations left the Czech leader Emil Hacha as State

President, von Neurath, who served as Hitler's personal representative, held all the real power.

Czechoslovakia had officially ceased to exist. The territory was divided into three pieces: the Protectorate of Bohemia and Moravia, the newly declared Slovak State, and the short-lived Republic of Carpathian Ukraine. The Czech leader Beneš would eventually go to London and form a government-in-exile, fully recognized by the Allies as a provisional government.[ix]

Jarmila and John now resided in Nova Paka, where she lived in terror of the Nazis as they marched throughout the small village, claiming ownership of whatever they desired. While Germany systematically gobbled up her homeland, the young mother prepared to welcome her second child. She was worried about their future, but John remained optimistic.

John placed his hand under her chin and tilted her face to look into her eyes.

"You mustn't show them any fear, Jarmila. They respect strength."

John's beautiful young wife was soft-hearted and kind, but she was also smart and resilient. He knew she could stand her own ground when necessary.

The Germans set about exploiting Czechoslovakia. On June 21, 1939, three months after his appointment as Reichsprotecktor, von Neurath issued a decree placing Jews under German jurisdiction and began confiscating their property. That same day, Jarmila gave birth to a son.

They named him Vladimir (also known as Lada, and later as Don). He was a sickly baby who suffered from asthma and cried often. The doctor told Jarmila the family should move across the ocean for Lada's health, but they were happy in the little Czechoslovakian village. John was delighted with the addition of a boy to the family, and two-year-old Eva loved the new baby. She brought soft toys to his crib and helped her mother entertain little Lada. Jarmila turned their ordinary daily tasks into playful games. Eva learned to help dress the baby and fold diapers. She spent hours talking to baby Lada, making funny faces, and tickling his toes.

On September 1, 1939, as Lada began to smile and coo, Hitler addressed the Reichstag to announce the invasion of Poland and the beginning of World War II. Czech Jews began being deported to Poland in October 1939.

Jarmila sewed outfits for her children, often using the same bolt of cloth to make a romper for Lada and a dress for Eva. She sang as she worked, her small fingers stitching straight seams into the fabric. When John arrived home, Eva raced to meet him at the door. Soon, Lada learned to sit up and then to crawl. The winter months passed quickly, with little intrusion from the outside world.

While Jarmila kept to herself in their Nova Paka home, John noticed daily changes in the economy. The German invasion was taking a financial toll, and Hitler urgently needed foreign currency to help pay the heavy cost of militarization. His solution was to establish an artificially high exchange rate between the Czechoslovak Koruna and the German Reichsmark—bringing consumer goods to Germans while it created shortages in the Czech lands. Blackouts and rationing were common.

For some, life became unbearable. After the Nazi takeover, many chose suicide as a way out. Like all Czechs, John and Jarmila had to apply for new identification documents as the Nazis forced them to declare they were not Gypsies or Jewish. They were also required to show authorities a family tree establishing their lineage back to their grandparents. No one could leave the Protectorate without a visa. Authorities executed many people, and a new rule required the deceased's relatives to pay for the executions and their announcements.[x]

Jarmila barely recognized their small town. Large swastika flags hung from the buildings and shops posted signs to proclaim they were Aryan. Hitler's SS guards, dressed totally in black, patrolled the streets, while German officers and soldiers rode in cars decorated with swastikas. Often, the exuberant teens in the Hitler Youth staged parades through the city.

During one blackout in Prague, defiant Czechs painted the letter "V" for victory on a few of the buildings. Taken by the symbol, the Nazis began to use the "V" for themselves. Soon, someone created a huge "V" on the cobblestones of Old Town Square.

Authorities confiscated and burned Bibles in the town square. Despite a ban on religion, people still found ways to worship. Czechoslovakia was a strong Catholic country at the time. Farmers had placed prayer sites in the middle of their fields, so the workers had a place to pray during the day.

John and Jarmila tried not to attract attention. They still hoped to raise their children in a free and independent Czechoslovakia and prayed the war would end soon. When Jarmila learned secondary schools would be required to use pro-Nazi textbooks, she was thankful her children were not yet in elementary school. But the Nazis were everywhere, and their rules scattered Jarmila's dreams of freedom into the wind.

The German occupation of the Sudetenland made life intolerable for many of the Czech people. The new laws restricted travel. No one could move about the country without a permit. In response, Czech families chose to ignore the formalities. They walked away from homes, farms, and businesses, leaving them to decay. Abandoned properties became a blight on the previously well-tended communities.

Even Jarmila defied the travel ban one Sunday morning. Homesick for her family, she packed diapers, clothing, and a lunch basket into a baby buggy and took her children for a walk to visit them. Three-year-old Eva walked alongside her mother, and baby Lada rode in the stroller. The journey took place under the unsuspecting noses of the German authorities.

With their invasion of Czechoslovakia in 1938, Germany had assumed control of the popular Czech-made Tatra car manufacturing plant, and gained access to Czech steel and chemical factories, as well as all their military weapons. Hitler used the weapons and ammunition to conquer Poland in 1939 and France in 1940—both countries who had pushed Czechoslovakia to surrender to Germany in 1938. Most Czech factories continued to produce machine guns, tanks and artillery—simply switching from Czech designs to German versions. They moved entire factories from Czechoslovakia and reassembled them in Linz, Austria.[xi]

Privately, John grumbled to Jarmila about the role Hitler forced their country to play in the war. "We were the first country Adolph Hitler annexed, but it wasn't to re-claim the German-speaking people. He wanted our factories and our weapons."

Jarmila sat at the mirrored vanity table and brushed her hair—one hundred strokes every night, just as she brushed Eva's to make it shine. "Speak softly, John. They have ears everywhere."

"It's true." John's lowered voice failed to conceal his anger. "Hitler gained more than a million rifles, 100,000 pistols, 43,000 machine guns, and 2,000 field cannons when he occupied Czechoslovakia, and that doesn't include one billion rounds of ammunition."

Jarmila shook her head. "No wonder he invaded us first."

John paced the floor as he talked. "Hitler made a speech about it. He said Germany wanted Czech tanks, anti-aircraft artillery pieces. Our weaponry was enough to arm half his army. We must remember what kind of man he is. He won't stop until he has all of Europe. And that includes stripping Czechoslovakia of our resources. We're already paying higher prices. Mark my words, Hitler will support his war on the backs of the Czech people."

Each day, the Nazis tightened their control over the Jews. In September 1941, they forced all Jews to wear the yellow star for identification. John and Jarmila watched as the town was divided between those with a star, and those without. Although they weren't Jewish, the young couple had become friends with merchants and townspeople who were.

Soon, many shop owners, neighbors and school children walked through the small village with downcast eyes, the stars boldly affixed to their clothing. Jarmila saw them on the streets and swallowed her normal greeting. It wasn't safe to acknowledge them any longer.

The Germans systematically destroyed synagogues and Jewish graveyards throughout the Sudetenland, sparing only the city of Prague. They planned to establish a Central Jewish Museum to display the property they had stolen from Jews whom they packed into overcrowded freight cars and deported to concentration camps.[xii]

Hitler assigned Reinhard Heydrich—the man with the iron heart—additional responsibilities in the region that was formerly known as Czechoslovakia. Trying to portray himself as a friend of the Czech working class, Heydrich, who now served as Deputy Protector of Bohemia and Moravia, took steps to alleviate the growing discontent. He increased rations for workers in the armaments industry, improved welfare services, and offered free shoes to Czech workers. For a brief period, he declared Saturday a holiday, reducing the workweek to five days.

Next, Heydrich restructured The National Union of Employees, making it more like the German Labor Front, with free concerts, films, and sporting events to win their favor. He staged a photo with a group of Czech workers on October 24, 1941, to demonstrate his concern for them. John and his business friends considered the gestures publicity stunts. They laughed when Heidrich later referred to his own policies as "optical effects" designed to improve morale and increase productivity. Meanwhile, wage increases failed to keep up with inflation, and the workers remained unhappy.[xiii]

When his efforts to win over the Czechs failed, Reinhard Heydrich reverted to his true colors. Under his leadership as head of the Nazi security services, Hitler's armies spread across the continent, clearing their own way through mass executions, torture, and intimidation. Stories of their cruelty reached Nova Paka, where Jarmila resolved to keep her children safe at home.

Jarmila, center, kept her children close to home in 1942. From left to right: Lada, Jarmila, and Eva. Jarmila is wearing the coat that would later conceal money and jewelry in the lining.

CHAPTER FIVE

STRUGGLING TO SURVIVE

1942-43

In spring of 1942, while she was pregnant with her third child, a tragedy hit so close to home that Jarmila would live in fear of the Germans for the rest of her life. Jarmila was twenty-one, a few months shy of her twenty-second birthday. Eva was five years old, and little Lada, three.

Eva peered out the window, watching for her daddy to come home, as she did every evening. John lifted her in a hug. "Where are Mommy and Lada?"

The little girl pointed to the kitchen.

"Let's go find them. It's time for supper."

Together, they walked through the arched threshold into a kitchen filled with the aroma of vegetable soup. The kitchen light cast a halo around Jarmila's blond hair, where she stood at the kitchen stove. Lada played on the rug at her feet. John's petite wife with her rounded belly was still the most beautiful woman he had ever known.

Jarmila ladled soup into their bowls, and the family joined hands around the table and bowed their heads. John lifted the spoon to his lips. Somehow, Jarmila had made a delicious meal from rationed chicken and a few of the remaining potatoes and carrots they had stored in the cellar from John's summer garden. Prices had continued to rise, and the German soldiers demanded more from the Czech people each day. That night, after they tucked the children into bed. John whispered to Jarmila. "I heard new rumors about Heydrich today."

"They can't be good," Jarmila said. "That man is evil."

By 1942, Heydrich had acquired two additional nicknames—The Butcher of Prague and the Hangman of Europe.

"He has earned his reputation." John took a slip of paper from his pocket and handed it to his wife.

Jarmila read the three words written there. "The Final Solution."

She looked up at John with a puzzled expression. "What does this mean?"

John leaned closer to whisper in her ear. "They plan to kill every Jew. More than 11 million throughout all of Europe and part of Russia."

Jarmila's hands flew to her face. "No!"

"Shhh," John motioned for her to lower her voice.

"The resistance is going to stop him."

Now Jarmila had more to worry about. She and John knew several members of the Czech and Slovak resistance movement. Over the next several weeks, they heard bits and pieces of the secret plan. A cadre of Czech soldiers went to Scotland to prepare for "Operation Anthropoid," the code name for a top-secret mission to assassinate Reinhard Heydrich.

After several months of training in marksmanship and explosives, the assassination team finished with paratrooper drills. At last, they were prepared to stage their attack. Two soldiers from the Czechoslovak army, Jan Kubis and Jozef Gabecki, volunteered for the mission. They understood they were not likely to survive, but they were determined to stop Heydrich. Impressed by their bravery, John whispered to Jarmila late into the night, explaining the planned attack.

"How do you know this?" Jarmila asked.

"I hear things in the village," John said.

"I wish you didn't."

"It's just news from friends of the resistance, eager to help our country."

"Still. It's dangerous," Jarmila said.

On May 27, 1942, Kubis and Gabecki, along with another soldier named Adolf Opalka, positioned themselves to assassinate Heydrich as his chauffeur-driven car rounded the bend of a curve. After all the planning, Gabecki's gun jammed, and the mission nearly failed. Heydrich and his chauffeur pulled the car to the side of the road and shot back. But Kubis acted quickly. He tossed a grenade at the car and wounded Heydrich. Flying shrapnel cut into Kubis, but he, Gabecki and Opalka made it to safety. They rushed Heydrich to a hospital, where he died eight days later, on June 4th.[xiv]

With his key security leader killed, Hitler was furious. He demanded retribution—first threatening to murder up to 10,000 Czechs. Rumors flew quickly through the Czech community. John and Jarmila pretended to know nothing about the assassination. While Hitler's SS officers investigated the assassination, Jarmila prayed they would find nothing that led them to Nova Paka. Even though she and John had no direct contact with the resistance soldiers, the Czech community was a close one. People often passed messages from hand-to-hand until they reached their destination. She had burned the note John handed her the day he told her about The Final Solution. She hoped all Czechs had been as careful to destroy any evidence.

Unfortunately, the SS search was thorough. One determined young officer uncovered a single letter where a soldier mentioned the town of Lidice. It was enough to fuel Hitler's wrath. He ordered the annihilation of all occupants. The little village, 22 kilometers northwest of Prague, was to be destroyed. The revenge was swift and violent.

Five days after Heydrich's death, on the night of June 9, SS officials and German police surrounded the little village. They separated the men (including boys over the age of 15) from the women and children. And the slaughter began. First, the Germans took the men to a local farmstead and shot 173 of them. They buried them in mass graves—five at a time, then ten at a time. They razed the town to the ground, diverted a river that used to run through the village, and destroyed everything in sight. Later, they executed another twenty townspeople at a shooting range near Prague.

A total of 203 women and girls over the age of 16 were deported to Ravensbruck concentration camp where 53 of them died before the end of the war. Nazis murdered 80 of the remaining children outright, gassing them at the Chelmno killing center.

They selected nine children with fair hair and blue eyes for Germanization and sent them to a group home in Poland. There, instructors taught them German, ultimately placing them with adoptive German parents.

Seven smaller children, under the age of one, were sent to a German orphanage in Prague. Another seven Lidice infants were born in the months that followed the town's annihilation—most of the newborn babies were also placed in orphanages. Of these fourteen very young children, eight survived the war.

Hitler was proud of the annihilation of Lidice, and the similar destruction of Lezaky, another small town destroyed as an example to others who might dare to resist German rule. Nazis filmed the carnage and forced people to watch it. The Lidice massacre took place on June 9-18, 1942. A resistance fighter betrayed his colleagues, and the seven parachutists hiding in Prague's Church of Saints Cyril and Methodius fought valiantly to the end.[xv]

On July 3, 1942, the Nazis humiliated 200,000 Czechs gathered on Wenceslas Square in Prague, forcing them to pledge their loyalty to the Reich and to give the Nazi salute. Four days later, on July 7, 1942, Jarmila gave birth to her second daughter, Vlasta.

As a mother of three children under the age of five, Jarmila worried that Hitler's bloodthirsty soldiers would come knocking on their door next. She gathered her children near and refused to let them out of her sight. The Lidice story hit too close to home. The small town was just 12 miles northeast of Prague, and only 90 miles from Nova Paka, where the Honolka's made their home. If this could happen to an entire town, what might the Germans do to her own children?

Her fear was justified. German troops made monthly searches of homes at random. Fully armed soldiers with barking dogs pounded on the front doors of targeted Nova Paka neighborhoods at all hours of the day or night. One night, just after midnight, the Nazis came to the Honolka house.

The soldiers pounded on the Honolkas' front door.

Jarmila woke to the sounds of crying. She ran to gather her children. Eva and Lada clung to her nightgown. She carried baby Vlasta in her arms.

"Öffne die Tür!" When the Nazis shouted the harsh words, John pulled on his pants and rushed to the door.

Two heavily armed soldiers lined the family against the wall and held them at gunpoint while others searched the house. Staring into the barrels of those guns, Jarmila and the children were terrified. If the Nazis discovered anything suspicious—radios, ammunition or extra food—the penalty was immediate death.

The raid lasted only minutes, but the men left Jarmila's neat little house in disarray. John and Jarmila were grateful the Nazis missed two items in their search: a radio hidden in the attic, and a small piece of black-market meat John had secretly purchased from a farmer.

"It was all for show, Jarmila," John said. "They only wanted to frighten us."

Tears trickled from Jarmila's eyes. After Lidice and the Nazi raid of her own home in Nova Paka, the young mother feared Hitler more than ever, becoming cautious of all German people.

CHAPTER SIX

LIFE UNDER THE NAZI REGIME

In the spring of 1943, John and Jarmila tried to give their children a normal life. Eva was five years old, Lada, three and a half. At eight months, baby Vlasta was constantly happy. She learned to crawl and was delighted with everything she saw. All the children enjoyed the outdoors. On warm spring days, Jarmila often spread a blanket on the grass where they could turn their faces to the sun while she read to them.

Eva played "Princess of the Meadow," dancing through the fields where dandelions (Pampelisky) bloomed. She picked the flowers and intertwined the stems to make necklaces, bracelets and rings. Gathering a basketful of the bright yellow flowers, she twisted clusters of them into a crown to place on her head. Jarmila smiled at her flower child.

She curled Eva's blond hair into ringlets that framed her face and hung to her shoulders. "You look like a Sun Princess," she said.

"Ne, Maminko. (No, Mother.) I am a ballerina."

"One day, we will enroll you in a ballet class so you can dance on a stage," Jarmila said. "You will be in the spotlight, twirling on your toes."

"The sun is my spotlight," Eva said, as she whirled in circles around her mother.

Jarmila told her stories about symphony concerts and the Czech National Ballet. She showed her daughter pictures of real ballerinas and described the beautiful costumes they wore. Over time, Eva came to love and appreciate the arts, just like her mother. It was an idyllic time, amid their dismal surroundings.

As political conditions worsened in 1943, the Czechoslovak resistance forces regrouped and began intense guerrilla warfare activities against the Germans. John heard rumors of their efforts and assured Jarmila the war would soon be behind them.

"The resistance forces are preparing to assist the U.S. and the Soviet Union," he said. "Together, they will defeat the Germans."

"I hope it happens soon," Jarmila said. "Hitler's soldiers have closed many shops and the ones remaining will soon have empty shelves."

John's hoped-for defeat of the Nazis did not come true that summer, but Jarmila's dire prediction did. Additional stores closed, and food rations were more restricted than ever before. Families waited in long food lines, only to discover there was no food available by the time they reached the counter. Many turned to black-market sources.

John and Jarmila planted a garden to supplement their food rations. They raised fruits and vegetables—enough to cook for dinner, and extra for Jarmila to set aside for winter. She made jars of preserves and hid them inside the coal bin in a corner of the cool basement.

Eva was old enough to help with the garden. She loved the poppy seed patch, and the sweet pastries Jarmila baked with poppy seed filling. The six-year-old grew more independent each day. She had only two dresses, so Jarmila sewed beautiful pinafores to cover them. Each morning, Eva chose one of the frilly aprons to slip on over her dress. Jarmila tied a big ribbon around her daughter's waist, with a huge bow in the back. Eva adored the ruffled shoulders on the pinafores and pretended they were wings.

The little girl bounced with energy. While her father worked and her mother tended the younger children, Eva ran through the fields and climbed trees. She snuck into the poppy seed patch and broke off the pods, gobbling handfuls of the seeds—even when they were still green. The bitter taste appealed to her. She believed the poppy seeds made her stronger. Soon, she climbed higher in the trees.

Late in the afternoon, Eva scrambled down from a tree to return home, pinafore wings torn from her shoulders and the ribbon sash dragging behind her. Jarmila rolled her eyes when she saw her bedraggled little princess.

"It would be better to have ten boys than one girl," she said.

When John discovered Eva was the culprit who had eaten the green poppies, he scolded her, "We need the ripe black poppy seeds to top our breads, sweet breads and kolaches," he said. "Green poppy seeds are bad for you. And if you eat all the seeds now, we will have none for winter."

For good measure, he bent little Eva over his knee and swatted her bottom with his open palm. It was a lesson she would always remember.

In the fall of 1943, Eva attended public school, where the core curriculum aimed to indoctrinate students to a Nazi worldview. The six-year-old feared anyone wearing a uniform. She hid behind her mother's skirts if German soldiers approached. One afternoon, Jarmila heard the bombs dropping and raced to the school. She found Eva, cowering in the basement.

"The building was shaking, Maminko."

"It's over now." Jarmila smoothed her daughter's hair and held her close.

"Did our house fall down?"

"We're okay, Evičko. Come. I'll show you."

Eva clung to her mother's hand until they were safely home. The terror had subsided, for the moment, but it never truly disappeared.

For many days, the bombs fell—destroying some shops and blowing glass windows from the school building. Eva hid in the basement with her classmates; certain the rubble would bury them alive. When all was clear, the teachers directed the children back to their classrooms. Often, they dismissed class for the day. The children stayed where they were, crying at their desks, too afraid bombs would strike them on their way home.

Eva described her fears to her mother. "What if I come home and our house is gone? The Nazis will send me to live with Hitler."

"That will not happen," Jarmila said. "I will find you first."

But Jarmila knew there was truth at the heart of the little girl's terror. Blonde, blue-eyed children were part of the dictator's plan for a "perfect race."

Jarmila made the sign of the cross on her daughter's forehead before she sent her to school. "God will protect you. Come home safe."

Regularly, the Nazis held huge bonfires to burn books in the community—the classics and all inspirational books written to lift the human spirit. They searched for all Bibles and tossed them into the blaze. Religion was considered unnecessary in a world where the government meets the needs of the people. Hitler wanted a perfect race, mentally and physically; he would exterminate anyone who hindered his progress. Bibles served only to promote ideas of hope and fairness, which were contrary to the New Order.

John and his close friends gathered in the Honolka attic in secrecy when they could. With the windows tightly sealed so no light could leak through, they huddled around the forbidden radio. The men used candles for their meetings; no one was allowed to use electricity after 9 p.m. They tuned the radio to Radio Free Europe and listened to Prime Minister Churchill's confident voice telling them to "never, never, never give up."

The Bible was close at hand. The men took turns reading words of hope, courage, faith, and strength. Afterwards, everyone carefully avoided detection as they snuck home, staying in the shadows where they would not be seen. The curfew on the street was 9 p.m.; violation could result in serious consequences. After his friends slipped away, John hid the precious Bible and radio between the rafters in the attic until the next secret meeting.

Under the Nazis, the most important educational subjects were sports, history and racial science. Sports and physical fitness made up five hours of instruction every day. Religion was no longer offered in schools. Any textbooks used to educate students had to be approved by the party. The authorities dismissed all Jewish teachers, and teachers with undesirable political beliefs. Membership in the Nazi Party was compulsory for all teachers. Eva learned to obey her teachers and ask no questions. At home, Jarmila taught her to respect the Bible and keep it hidden from the Nazi officers, should they ever enter the Honolka home.

As the Nazis gathered prisoners and forced them to march through the streets, Jarmila felt compelled to help the captives. She gathered potatoes from the cellar, boiled them in a large pot, and carried the pot to the edge of the street. In direct defiance of the Nazi orders, Jarmila handed the hot potatoes to the hungry prisoners as they passed. One prisoner accepted the potato and gave her a ring he had made from a prison spoon. Jarmila's kindness landed her in prison. The Nazis confiscated the potatoes and put Jarmila in jail for a few days as punishment. Long afterward, Jarmila wondered about the fate of the unknown prisoner who had given her the spoon ring. She had lost the ring, but she never forgot the look on the man's face as he thanked her for the food.

The Nazis roared through the country at speeds up to 100-miles-per-hour in the sleek Czechoslovakian-made Tatra car they had commandeered shortly after Germany first invaded, while their soldiers hauled innocent people away to concentration camps. John described the officers to Jarmila as "crazy drivers."

"Their egos will get them killed," he said.

Over time, hundreds of Nazi officers—lured by the aerodynamic style of the popular car—lost control of the heavy vehicles when they attempted sharp turns at high speeds. So many were killed in car accidents that the Allied forces began to refer to the Tatra as the "Czech Secret Weapon."[xvi]

The next spring, President Beneš partnered with the Soviets hoping to free his country from the Nazis. On May 8, 1944, Beneš signed an agreement with Soviet leaders stipulating that "Czechoslovak territory liberated by Soviet armies" would be placed under Czechoslovak civilian control.

From August through October, the Czech resistance intensified its activity, culminating in an armed attack of the Rebel Slovak Army against the German Wehrmacht forces. People called it The Slovak National Uprising (The "1944 Uprising") The battle centered on Banská Bystrica, 200 miles southeast of Nova Paka, where John and Jarmila lived.

By late August, the German troops had handily disarmed the Eastern Slovak Army, weakening the entire Slovak Army. The Nazi forces sent many of the rebel soldiers to concentration camps. Those who escaped joined other partisan units and rallied against the Germans again, as the fighting continued.

On September 21, Czechoslovak troops formed in the Soviet-liberated village of Kalinov, located in the northeastern part of the country. Soviet troops (the Red Army) occupied most of Slovakia and the Czech lands, supported by Czech and Slovak resistance troops, from the east to the west. The Allied forces had not yet made their way into Czechoslovakia.[xvii]

CHAPTER SEVEN

DESPERATE TIMES

For families like the Honolka's, the war created further hardships. The authorities allowed them only a half pound of meat per person, per month, and one dozen eggs. But, even with food stamps, it was impossible to buy food that didn't exist. Store shelves were often empty in Czechoslovakia. Prices skyrocketed. Bribery was rampant. Starving families resorted to whatever means they could find, to feed their families. When coffee was scarce, they boiled the taproots of chicory—along with concoctions of soybeans, barley, and grains—into a dark liquid substitute.

Often, the only meat available was horse, which was muscular and tough. In contrast, a cow's stomach was a delicacy. People used all parts of an animal to feed their families. Jarmila sliced the lining of the cow's stomach into long strips of tripe—which resembled noodles—and used them to prepare "Dršťková Polévka" Soup. Though little Vlasta loved the combination of tripe, onions, marjoram, paprika, and garlic, Eva hated the taste. When she saw her mother preparing the soup, the little girl hid under her bed or pretended to be too ill to eat.

Inspectors checked the Honolka home once or twice each month, to ensure compliance with food rations. The trick to getting products was to have connections—either to a producer of goods or to a storekeeper. Fortunately for the Honolka family, John was a master at networking and connections. He always seemed to find a food source when they needed it most.

One week, when John and Jarmila had skipped all their own meals to feed their children, John came home with dark circles under his eyes.

"I have found a farmer willing to sell us the stomach of his cow," he said.

Jarmila shook her head. "It's too dangerous."

"The children need meat."

"They need their father more."

"I'll go after dark."

That night, John slipped out of their house after midnight.

At 5 a.m. the next morning, Jarmila heard the heavy knock on the door. Two Nazi officers shoved their way inside, their German Shepherd dog snarling beside them. It was another spontaneous raid. The family members lined up against their living room wall with their hands behind them.

Eva fidgeted with fear. The dog growled and bared his teeth.

The officers searched the house, opening drawers and stomping in the attic overhead. They checked behind the cushions on the couch and lifted mattresses in the bedrooms. They returned to confront John for the food stamp records. With the report in hand, they headed to the kitchen pantry. The room was windowless. Cool and dark. Without an icebox, it was the only place they could store foods that might spoil at normal room temperatures.

The hair on the back of Eva's neck stood on end, sending a shiver down her spine. She had heard her parents arguing the night before.

The search didn't take long. The Nazis discovered the cow's stomach in the Honolka pantry. They carried the package and shook it in John's face.

One soldier pointed a rifle at Jarmila and the children.

The other held John at gunpoint. "Where did you get the meat?"

John stood silently.

The soldier whipped his pistol across John's face. John fell to his knees.

"You will tell us, or we will shoot you, your wife and all of your children."

Jarmila pleaded with her husband. "You have to tell them!"

When John gave the farmer's name, the soldiers marched John and Jarmila to a military truck at gunpoint. They drove the truck to the farmer's house, arrested him, and dragged him into his barn, along with his wife, and John and Jarmila.

"Now, you will see what happens to those who disobey our orders," the officer shouted.

The Nazis forced John, Jarmila, and the farmer's wife to watch as they strung a rope over a high beam and wrapped a noose around the farmer's neck. Securing the rope, they suspended the man until he hanged to death. The man died because he tried to help others.

John returned to his own family overwhelmed with guilt. Jarmila tried to soothe him.

"The man was hung because we wanted to eat," John said. "This is my fault."

"No. The Nazis are to blame."

Jarmila's words could not ease his conscience. The event haunted John. He moaned in his dreams and woke, shaking from the terror of the memory. Nothing could erase the image of the farmer hanging dead in his barn. It was a burden of guilt he would carry the rest of his life.

Although the Czech resistance movement was growing, they had made little progress until early in 1945, when partisan forces in Czechoslovakia numbered roughly 7,500 people. The Allied armies were closing in, and resistance fighters saw their momentum as an opportunity to act. It was a winter of discontent. Czechoslovakians struggled to survive. Some women became pregnant to escape the long hours in the factories. Many lost hope and turned to suicide.

Workers doubled their hours or took on extra jobs. Even at 64 hours a week and 10 hours on Sunday, they couldn't keep up with inflation. Food costs put fresh fruits and vegetables out of reach, creating a health crisis. Poor nutrition and stress resulted in a surge of infectious diseases across the country.[xviii]

Amidst all this upheaval, news arrived that Hitler threatened to annihilate the Czechs' beloved capital city of Prague. Czech nationals were furious. On April 4, 1945, under a new provisional Czechoslovak government, the Soviet Red Army took over the administration for the Czech towns—expelling the

Germans and forming "National Committees" to assume control of each town. By the war's end, the Soviets had created nearly 5,000 committees.

Like most Czechs, John and Jarmila welcomed the changes. They wanted the Nazis out of their cities. "The momentum has turned," John said. "This time, the resistance movement cannot fail."

The turmoil came to a head one month later, on May 5. The Czechs had reached their limit. In a spontaneous battle known as the "Prague Uprising," they rallied to fight the Germans who occupied their city. Early that morning, Czech police officers burst into a radio station and began fighting with the SS troops who occupied the building. Czech broadcasters heard the commotion in the hallways and called for citizens to revolt against the Nazis.

Thirty thousand Czech men and women poured into the streets of Prague, determined to reclaim their freedom. In a rally of national pride, they rebelled against the Nazis through hundreds of small actions. Czech citizens destroyed German street signs. They defiantly flew Czech flags from their windows and stood together against the Germans. Tram conductors refused to accept German Reichsmarks as payment or to announce the stops in German. By the end of the first day, the Czechs had resumed control of their bridges, the railway stations and the broadcasting building. Overnight, they constructed over 1,600 barricades.

German troops responded by sending 40,000 troops to Prague. Armed with aircraft, tanks and artillery, they bombed the city, claiming 1,200 lives. The explosions hit civilian apartments and knocked down the barricades. Despite damage to the radio broadcasting building and a bleak outlook, the Czechs kept fighting.

Then, in a surprise show of support, the Russian Liberation Army (ROA), a German army unit made up of Soviet POWs, switched sides to join the Czech defenders. The battle continued for only a day before the Nazi's announced an unconditional surrender to the Allied forces in France. Tired of fighting, the ROA abandoned Prague to surrender to the US Army.

Outnumbered and alone, the Czechs faced the Germans on their own. In

Prague, the Nazis refused to follow their country's lead and surrender. Instead, they fought harder, pushing the Czechs back again. They crashed through the barricades, using civilians as human shields along the way.

On May 8, 1945, the Germans launched another attack. They were successful: taking the Masaryk rail station and murdering 50 captured Czech fighters. Finally, both sides negotiated a ceasefire.[xix] The Germans retreated on May 9, but not before they launched an incendiary shell that seriously damaged the Old Town Hall of Prague, with its beloved tower and astronomical clock.

Fire burned the figures of the apostles on the astronomical clock and most of the exterior decoration, and the clock mechanism was broken. (Note: It wasn't until 1948 that the astronomical clock began operating again, featuring new figures of the apostles made by Vojtěch Sucharda. At that time, the bell and drum mechanism were set to Central European Time.) In retaliation for the damages to their Old Town Hall and tower, and the partial destruction of the astronomical clock, the Czech fighters hanged Germans from lampposts and burned their bodies.[xx]

On the morning of May 9, German forces exited Prague. Later that day, the Soviet Red Army arrived in Prague and put down any remaining German units in the city. Czech citizens flooded the streets to welcome the Red Army and celebrate their liberation.

At last, the war was over. In May 1945, just after Eva's eighth birthday, Czechoslovak troops took possession of the borderland. The leadership formed an administrative commission composed exclusively of Czechs.

After World War II, Czechoslovakia had looked favorably on the Russians, who had liberated them. When the Soviet troops began to withdraw from the country in July of 1945, Czechoslovakia—like most of the Slavic states in post-war Europe—became a "satellite state" of the Soviet Union. They regained control of their own government but remained heavily influenced by the Soviet Union.

In 1945, Edvard Beneš, the head of the Czech government who had been exiled to London during the war, returned to his native land to lead the new national government. Now it was time to remove the Germans from their country. President Beneš proposed a "humane and orderly transfer" of the German population during a July address to the Potsdam Conference—including the U.S., Britain, and the Soviet Union.

By August of that year, working under Potsdam guidelines, authorities deported between 700,000 and 800,000 Sudeten Germans from the Czechoslovakian borderlands to Germany. Czechoslovak politicians encouraged the expulsions; local authorities, primarily groups of armed volunteers, carried out the orders. About 244,000 ethnic Germans—some crucial for industries, some anti-fascists, and some married to ethnic Czechs—were allowed to remain in Czechoslovakia.

The expulsions continued through the fall of 1946, with an estimated 1.6 million deported to the American zone (to become West Germany), 800,000 to the Soviet zone (to become East Germany). Many of the deportees died from hunger, illness, violence or suicides.[xxi]

CHAPTER EIGHT

THE WAR IS OVER

At the close of the war in 1945, John came to Jarmila with excitement in his eyes. "I want to start my own business, making oplatky (wafers) to have as a treat with coffee, tea or ice cream. I've found a building available in Pilnikov that would make a nice factory."

John had worked in a chocolate factory when he first met Jarmila. There, he had been successful at sales and distribution. He believed he could succeed as an independent business owner. Jarmila smiled at his enthusiasm. The wafers he described were already popular in Europe. She knew her husband was a visionary who would work hard to succeed.

As Russian and American troops left the city, they abandoned many vehicles. John purchased a 1939 Ford the American military had left behind. He drove it to and from his shop in Pilnikov, just 4.5 miles from their home in Trutnov.

He named the business "Koruna" (Crown)" and soon became known for his creative offerings—particularly his flavorful original wafer, called the "Oplatky." Nearly eight inches around, the pastry was made of many thin layers of dough, filled with cream filings, nuts, chocolate, caramel, and sugar. John made them in vanilla, lemon, chocolate, hazelnut, and almond. He knew customers were likely to purchase more than one, simply to compare the lemon with the chocolate, or the vanilla with the hazelnut.

While John grew his business in Pilnikov, the Communists expanded their power in Czechoslovakia. With the economy spiraling out of control, it was no surprise when the elections of 1946 favored Communist Party candidates. Voters saw Communism as the answer to their economic woes.

The Communist Party made huge electoral gains, and the Czech President Edvard Beneš formed a coalition with them in his administration. Although Czechoslovakia was not formally within the Soviet orbit, the Communists had taken over many seats in their national assembly. By 1946, Communists held significant positions in the Czechoslovak government.

Jarmila, happily pregnant with their fourth child, barely noticed the power shifts within the Czech government. For her, the war had ended. The Nazis had gone. She focused on raising her family in the country she loved. Eva and Lada were already in school, and Vlasta wasn't far behind them.

On Saturday, June 8, 1946, she and John welcomed John Jr. into the world. Eva, at nine, adored the new baby. Lada, who would turn seven the following month, was excited to have a brother. Vlasta, almost four, announced that she was no longer the "baby" of the family—a fact she shared with anyone who would listen.

During the next two years, John and Jarmila enjoyed the benefits of owning a business. His innovative ideas and hard work paid off. He delivered his "Oplatky" desserts to retail stores across Czechoslovakia. Suddenly, it became a favorite at afternoon teas, as well as an evening dessert. Happy customers told their friends about the "Oplatky," and the factory flourished. When his sales continued to grow, John increased his staff to handle the volume.

John loved the business. He invested in equipment and his employees. By 1947, the factory had achieved the level of success John had always dreamed of—he was a man with an idea that had found its time. Now, his growing business provided delectable treats for his customers to sell, jobs for his assistants, and the good things of life for his family. John's friends and family were proud of his accomplishments. Before long the factory employed 25 people. John wore his success with humility.

"Any man can build a business if he is willing to take the risk," he told Jarmila. "All it takes is personal initiative, self-reliance, and hard work."

Jarmila smiled up at him. "Not every man will work as hard as you do, John."

That spring, loud claps of a thunderstorm woke them during the night. Lightning crackled across the sky, jagged streaks against the towering clouds. The phone rang early the next morning.

John hung up from the call and turned to face Jarmila. "It's bad news. A lightning bolt hit the factory. The building burst into flames. Half is gone."

"Destroyed?"

"The building. Our inventory and supplies. I'll go see what can be done."

That night, he returned with a new plan. "We will begin again," he said.

John's reputation for honesty and integrity proved to be an asset. The bank agreed to loan him money to rebuild the factory.

The joy people felt at the end of the war gradually disappeared as a different political, and economic climate emerged. It was 1947. The United States introduced the U.S. Marshall Plan, designed to help post-war European countries rebuild. When the Czech government moderates proposed that the country participate, the Communists adamantly opposed. They staged strikes and protests and led violent demonstrations the police could not control.

John told Jarmila about the riots one evening after dinner. "They say the Communists can't be stopped by anyone but the army—but it is run by General Svoboda, and he's a Communist himself."

"What about President Beneš? Can't he direct the army to stop the demonstrations?" Jarmila asked the same question that many Czechs raised.

"Not likely. He's too afraid the Soviets might return, or the country will get into a civil war."

That winter, the violence continued. Unable to control the demonstrations peacefully, the police resorted to extreme measures. Most were Communist sympathizers who grew weary of the protesters who opposed Communism. Stories of their cruelty raged throughout the country. Every day brought new atrocities to light.

John carried the news home to Jarmila one cold February night. "Students were demonstrating in the name of democracy on Nerudova

Street in Prague yesterday. When they refused to leave the streets, the police overpowered the young patriots and beat them into submission."

"Oh, no!" Jarmila was stunned.

"Last week, Nosek fired all the non-Communists who were still serving as police officers," John said. "The democratic ministers have demanded that eight of those officers be reinstated. Now, it's up to the ministers to vote."

The standoff escalated over the next two weeks. After a majority of the cabinet voted in favor of reinstating the non-Communist senior police officers, Nosek flatly refused. Twelve non-Communist ministers resigned their positions in protest.

Like other Czechs, John was surprised and dismayed by their resignations. He paced the floor of their kitchen, where he and Jarmila talked about the rapidly deteriorating turn of events. "Now the Communists have no one left in the cabinet to battle against them."

"Surely President Beneš will refuse to accept the resignations," Jarmila said. "That would keep a balance in the government."

"It would require more courage than he has shown, so far," John said.

At first, it seemed Jarmila's hopes would be realized. Although Beneš didn't refuse the resignations, he insisted on including ministers from non-Communist parties in the formation of any new government. But the Communist-led demonstrations accelerated, and Beneš—afraid of inciting a full insurrection that might give the Red Army an excuse to invade the country—backed down.

By April, the situation was worse. John saw the handwriting on the wall. "There's no way to stay neutral with the Communists. Beneš is giving them too much power. It won't end well." He was right.

Beneš gave in to Communist demands and handed his cabinet over to the party. In May, they held rigged elections and declared a Communist victory. Immediately, they fired thousands of people and arrested hundreds more. Beneš resigned on June 2, 1948, and Czechoslovakia, until then the last democracy in Eastern Europe, became a single-party state. The Communist

Party of Czechoslovakia, with Soviet backing, assumed undisputed control over the government of Czechoslovakia.[xxii]

Almost overnight, John and Jarmila noticed a new undercurrent of fear in their village. Suddenly, friends were distrustful of friends, brothers turned against brothers, and neighbors against neighbors as Communists took over the Czech government. John had become a capitalist in a Communist land, and his success was both envied and discouraged.

The Honolka family watched as their country succumbed to Communist rule. Russians who had helped them defeat the Nazis had now claimed the country for their own. Citizens of Czechoslovakia were forced to integrate with the new system.[xxiii] Those who failed to embrace Communism were monitored and questioned. If the Czech citizens resisted Communism, they could be subjected to house searches, imprisonment or execution—all without a trial.

The Russians took over where the Germans left off. Most of the soldiers were from the poor sections of their country. They pillaged, raped, and abused anyone who stood in their way. If anyone wore a watch, the soldiers confiscated it—many wore multiple watches on their arms as trophies.

In a large meadow behind the Honolka home, the Russians established a military camp. Every evening, the soldiers lit large bonfires, sang haunting melodies, drank vodka and performed Kozak dances. Eva watched out her window one night, mesmerized by the silhouettes of the Russian soldiers, dancing with the flames behind them.

Jarmila discovered her daughter at the window, tears streaming down her face. She knelt beside her. "Why are you crying?"

"For the horses," Eva said. "They were tied to the trees, and the soldiers beat them with sticks. Now they have foam coming from their mouths, but the soldiers ride them in circles around the field. I'm afraid they will die."

Jarmila hugged her daughter close. "You have a kind heart, Eva. We can't change what the soldiers do. But we can hope the horses will survive."

"Why do the Russians do it?"

"Because they can."

"If I ever have a horse, I will be good to it," Eva said.

"You should always choose good over evil," her mother replied.

Jarmila tucked her ten-year-old daughter back into bed, but the boisterous partying continued until early morning. With the break of dawn, the fields were quiet behind their house. She looked out the window and saw the horses standing tied to the trees once again.

The secret police planted bugs in private homes to record conversations that disparaged the government. They carried out unwarranted investigations on civilians who showed signs of opposing the regime.

Censorship became law. Radio broadcasts shared only positive propaganda about the regime and silenced any newspapers and magazines that criticized it. Communist officials could confiscate whatever they wanted "for the good of the state."

Residents of German descent, regardless of how long they had lived in Czechoslovakia, were ordered to leave the country, because of the atrocities the Nazis committed. Age was of no consideration. John's father was Austrian, and his mother was half German. They could not remain. They were told to pack 60 kilos of their possessions each (approximately 132 pounds per person). On the appointed day, a government truck picked up the two senior citizens and whisked them away into the unknown. Many weeks later, their letter arrived: they had been relocated to a two–room apartment in Berchtesgaden, Germany—nearly a 7-hour drive from Trutnov.

The government edicts were clear. Everyone was required to work. Disincentives stifled the work ethic; they discouraged innovations in the workplace. Manual laborers were paid higher wages than white-collar workers, as inexperienced tradesmen headed government-owned companies, while menial jobs were assigned to highly educated people. Instead of building a sense of "communal pride," the system resulted in jealousy and animosity.[xxiv]

The bakery factory owned by John Honolka in Pilnikov, Czechoslovakia (front and back views).

CHAPTER NINE

THE BUSINESS IS AT RISK

As Communism swept the country, John became more convinced that someone would take his factory from him. He believed it was only a matter of days, or weeks, before someone would complain about his success. Russian officials stared at John's business from across the street. He felt their presence behind him as he walked into the building each morning, and when he returned home at night. After several days of clandestine surveillance, a uniformed officer stood in front of John's desk at the factory one morning.

"The soldiers have decided your wife will be required to cook one meal each week for our officers," he said. "You will invite our officers to dinner."

John had expected to have his factory confiscated. Instead, the soldiers intended to invade his home, sit at his table and have Jarmila serve them. Refusal was not an option.

When John told Jarmila the Russians expected her to prepare a formal meal for them each week, Jarmila ran to their bedroom in tears.

He tried to reassure her. "This is a good thing, Jarmila. They will provide the meat for you to cook. Maybe they will begin to see us as we are—a young couple, raising children in a happy home. It will be more difficult for them to picture us as their enemy."

From that moment forward, Jarmila straightened her back, held her head high, and smiled as she prepared home-cooked food for the Communist soldiers. She lit the candles and poured their vodka. Trembling inside, Jarmila overcame her fear and grasped the platters of food in her shaking hands to set them firmly on the table in front of their guests. Together, she and John pretended to welcome the Communists into their home.

The Russians expected John and Jarmila to celebrate with them, drinking vodka in a toast to their victory over the Nazis. They wanted more guests invited to the party. One evening, Jarmila's sister, Maria, came to help prepare the meal. The soldiers insisted she join them in the toast. She declined.

"Unfortunately, I am allergic to alcohol," Maria said.

Insulted, the Russians forced her to participate. She swallowed the drink, but quickly became ill and lapsed into a coma. While the soldiers laughed, Jarmila called for an ambulance. John distracted the men long enough for the medics to arrive and rush his unconscious sister-in-law to the hospital.

The dinners continued as long as the soldiers occupied the city, but Jarmila's sister did not return. Maria could not endure another episode of alcohol poisoning. For a while, John's hospitality and Jarmila's smile were enough to keep the Russians satisfied.

Although Jarmila forced herself to remain calm when the Communists came for dinner, she struggled to find quality food to serve with the meat they brought. As the cost of living skyrocketed, food rations were strictly controlled. Shelves at Jarmila's local market were often bare. The Czechs paid more for less. She knew John did his best to supplement their rations with vegetables from his garden, but it wasn't enough.

Under Communist rule, the rich were declared enemies of the state. No farmer could own more than 120 acres of land, which destroyed their livelihood and jobs. Wealthy farmers, referred to as "kulaks," were blackmailed and threatened with imprisonment if they refused to join cooperatives. Those who resisted soon found themselves without supplies. The Communist regime rewarded those farmers who accepted leadership positions on the cooperative's committees; they received all-expenses-paid vacations abroad.

That September, President Beneš died. John and Jarmila were among the silent crowd who attended his public burial service. Along with other patriots, they mourned both the death of the popular leader and the demise of the democracy he represented.

In 1948, the factory had grown to be the largest independently owned business in the village. Inevitably, John's thriving business caught the attention of the government. One evening after the Russians had enjoyed another meal at the Honolka home, John spoke to Jarmila at bedtime. He wanted to prepare her for the worst-case scenario.

"These officers are not our friends," John said. "I see them hovering around the factory. They are up to something. They will find a way to take the business from me. If I'm arrested and we are separated, you must bring the children to Salzburg. We will find each other there. The city is under French rule, so we will be safe. I've already spoken to your brother. He will travel to Austria, too. We're arranging transportation through the underground network. Two will take us to Hungary, then two others to the Austrian border. There's a woman there who will help us."

"When?"

"When the time is right."

Two weeks later, John went into the hospital to have his tonsils removed. After several years of seasonal sore throats, the time had finally come when his doctor insisted it was time to perform the operation. After the procedure, John developed an infection. He was away from the factory for three weeks— long enough for the government to seize his records. John returned to find a Communist official waiting for him.

The officer sat in John's chair and motioned for him to take a seat in the visitor's chair. John refused the offer. "I believe I'll stand, if you don't mind."

"Whatever you prefer."

"How can I assist you?" John asked.

"It is I who must assist you, now, as we assume control of this business."

John raised an eyebrow but made no comment.

"Under Communism, no man should own so much or control this many workers. This is only permitted to the government." The officer spoke in a measured, authoritarian tone as he delivered the devastating news. "Today, this factory becomes the property of the state. You no longer own the business. We want you to show us how to manage it.

John stood a little taller and asked, "I would be paid as an employee to manage my own business?"

The officer tilted his head. "It will be a reasonable amount. I encourage you to accept this offer."

John refused and walked away from the factory. The next day, Sunday, police arrested him in a nearby park, in front of his family. They gave him one week to get his affairs in order before sending him to work in the coal mines. Instead, he spent the week planning his escape. He contacted underground resistance workers and made his way to Vienna.

As soon as he crossed the border into safety, John feared for the family he had left behind. He missed Jarmila and their children; his conscience prodded him to return home where he could plan an escape for the entire family. It was a noble goal, but the Communists anticipated his actions.

Once again, John was arrested and detained for three days, while the police attempted to coerce him into pledging allegiance to Communism. They hung John by his wrists and beat his back with leather straps. Eventually, the authorities released him on the condition that he return to the factory—the government, unable to manage the business, insisted that John teach them.

A few days later, another event brought John into the Communist spotlight. This time, it was a children's spat in the neighborhood. During an exchange with another child, taunting turned into name calling. Little Eva resorted to the most demeaning title her thought process could conjure up. "You, you, *Communist* you!"

Within hours, John Honolka was taken into custody for interrogation. He was thrown into jail on charges of indoctrinating his children against Communism and its benefits. When John still refused to become a Communist, he was charged with "illegal activities against the government and not cooperating in the best interest of society and state."

Officially declared an enemy of the state, John remained in prison for another three days while the police beat him, interrogated him, and ultimately deemed him "politically unreliable." Jarmila and her children clung to each other, terrified they would be next. Once again, the attempt to persuade John to embrace Communism failed. The Communists determined John would need to be "reeducated" over time. For now, they needed him at the factory until they could train others to run the business,

Upon his release from prison, John went home to Jarmila.

She hovered near the front door of their home, waiting. At last, she saw a man approaching from a distance, his coat collar pulled up around his neck. She threw open the door and ran to him.

She wrapped her arms around him and squeezed. Jarmila's eyes turned to steel. "They can't do this."

John finally spoke, his words muffled through swollen lips. "It seems they already have, Jarmila."

She rushed her husband to their kitchen where she nursed his wounds, tenderly dabbing away dried blood and applying cold compresses to his face. She crushed aspirin into a cup of hot tea and raised it to his lips. Then she put him to bed and sat by his side until he slept.

When the sun came up, she was still there.

John opened his eyes and looked up at her.

"As an enemy of the state, I will be under constant supervision," he said. "We have to escape."

Jarmila clenched her jaw and nodded.

CHAPTER TEN

THE ESCAPE

It was mid-September 1948. John and Jarmila returned to their normal routine, pretending to be obedient to the Communist rules. Jarmila prepared a meal for the Russian officers, as usual. They invited no one else into their home.

The children were allowed to play in the yard after school. Jarmila supervised them and shooed them into the house long before dinnertime. She and John spoke cautiously in their home. They walked outside to share a few minutes of conversation, careful not to break the curfew rules or rouse the suspicions of prying eyes. John resumed his job at the factory, where he interacted with his employees in a more subdued way.

One night, John came home to find Jarmila sewing the lining of her coat. She bent over the fabric, making tiny stitches to blend into the existing pattern.

Conscious that their home may be bugged, John kept his tone casual. "Time to mend the old coat, I see."

"Yes. I want it to hold together for another winter, so I'm patching the torn spots. Take off your coat and I will repair it tonight as well."

"Thank you, Jarmila. We can't afford new ones."

John handed her his coat, along with a small drawstring bag he had hidden in the waistband of his pants. "I stopped at the market for the needles and thread you requested."

Jarmila set the bag on her lap, removed a handful of currency, and tucked the money into a fold in her seam. She repeated the process for several hours that evening, hiding cash and gold jewelry to barter, and chocolate bars for energy food, into the linings of their coats. All the while, they spoke as though she were mending the worn coat fabric and darning socks.

"This is the time of year when the weather can change at any moment. You should keep your coat with you. I don't want you to catch a cold before winter even arrives."

"That's just as true for you, Jarmila."

"Yes. I know," she said. "And I'll remind the children, too."

Another night, John mentioned Jarmila's brother. "Olda stopped by the factory today. He looked good."

"The children miss their uncle," Jarmila said.

"He promised to visit soon."

"Did he mention Maria?"

"Your sister is doing well but will not come with him. She promises to visit later, perhaps in the spring."

Jarmila understood the meaning behind John's words. Her brother, Olda, wanted to escape with them. Maria would stay behind to watch over their parents.

The third week of September, John walked in the door casually, as always. He turned up the radio and whispered to Jarmila.

"Hurry. We go tonight. We must gather a few things and get the children to safety."

"Where are we going?"

"To Hungary. Olda arranged a driver. He will get us to the border."

He lowered the radio volume again and resumed a normal tone. "The evenings are cooler now, just as you predicted."

"Still, fall is my favorite time of year. The moon always seems brighter," Jarmila said.

John forced a chuckle. "You'll have to wait till Saturday to see the full moon you love."

It was a Friday night. John hoped the Communist officials would be preoccupied with weekend activities, leaving fewer of them on patrol. When the moon rose shortly after midnight, it would provide enough light to illuminate the rough ground, but not so much to expose the family. If they could sneak through the shadows to the edge of the city before midnight, they could reach the car that idled behind a warehouse.

As dusk fell, Jarmila dressed the children in warm clothes and tucked them into bed at the normal time.

Vlasta gave her sister a puzzled look. "Why am I wearing this to bed?"

"We're going on an adventure," Eva said. "I'll wake you in a few hours... but you must be very quick, and very quiet."

At eleven p.m., a patrol car drove slowly past the Honolka home. The neighborhood was silent. All the lights were out, as required by curfews. John peered out a corner of the window shade and watched the car turn at the corner. Jarmila and the children huddled together on the floor without a peep. If the house was under surveillance, any unusual sound might alert the guards to their plans. The taxi arrived in the dark a few minutes later.

When John saw the car turn, he signaled to Jarmila. John carried two-year-old John Jr. in his arms as he crept out of their side door and to the front. Eva crouched to follow in his footsteps. Lada and Vlasta stayed in a single file behind her. Jarmila trailed behind them, her heart pounding.

Jarmila's brother, Olda, was in the back seat of the car. Jarmila and Eva crawled in beside him. Lada sat on Olda's lap, and Vlasta on Jarmila's. John crowded into the front with the driver and held John Jr. in his lap.

"Did you get the identification papers?" John asked.

Olda opened his coat and patted a fat envelope tucked into his pocket. "Right here. These will get us across the border. They aren't real names, of course. But the age should be close enough. I'll sort them when we can safely shine a light."

They had planned a route through Kaschau, Hungary, and Budapest to Austria. The drive took nearly seven hours. Each time they approached the outskirts of a village, the driver proceeded without headlights along less traveled country roads. Jarmila held her breath much of the way. The children slept. Only Eva remained alert, eyes searching the darkness for Hungarian border guards.

Shortly before their arrival at the Hungarian border, the driver pulled onto a dirt road that led to a long field to a farmstead. They came to a stop beneath the trees. The taxi driver said, "This is as far as I go. Across the field is the farmhouse where you need to go."

The family climbed out of the taxi. Olda pulled out the envelope and retrieved a flashlight from beneath the seat of the car. He shuffled through the papers, checking the names and ages on each one. Then he began again.

Olda's hands shook as he counted. He turned to John. "We're one document short."

"That's impossible." John said. "We paid for seven."

"This is my fault. I should have checked them at the handoff," Olda said.

John shook his head. "There wasn't time. You risked everything to pick them up."

Olda shoved the envelope into John's hands. "You go without me. I'll go back with this driver. You meet our next contact, up ahead."

"No. We all go together. If someone questions us, we will say we haven't yet received identification papers for Johnny."

"It's too risky. You and your family must go without me," Olda said. "I'll join you later."

John grabbed Olda by his shoulders. "If you don't come now, you may never get out."

Jarmila and Eva gathered the children into the shadows at the edge of the field. Jarmila swaddled John Jr. into a sling across her chest.

The night was pitch black as the family walked through the long field of cut wheat. No one was to speak, even in the darkness. The only sound was the crackling of dried wheat as they walked silently through the stubble.

The family made their way by foot across the field to an old farmhouse where a large woman greeted them warmly. But luck was not with them that morning. The Hungarian woman refused their paperwork. "It will not pass inspection," she said.

Immediately, she called out to the police, who were nearby. "Over here! They are trying to escape."

The arrest was quick. The officers aimed their pistols at the family. John raised his hands in the air. Jarmila stood beside him. "We have children here," she shouted.

The officer's eyes flicked to the baby Jarmila carried in her arms.

Eva, Lada, and Vlasta lined up between John and Jarmila.

Their effort to escape had failed.

CHAPTER ELEVEN

JARMILA IN PRISON

Police arrested the family and took them to the city jail, where they locked them in a small, bare room. They huddled together on the floor of the cold cell, awaiting their fate. They slept fitfully on the floor until the guards returned.

At last, they unlocked the cell and escorted the family to a waiting convoy of vehicles. Olda stood handcuffed beside one of them. Guards separated the family into three groups. They shoved John into the rear of a police wagon and directed nine-year-old Lada to the car with Olda. Jarmila and the other three children—Eva, Vlasta and John Jr.—crowded into a third vehicle.

Hours later, they arrived at Moson Yintin Tolinshaus Prison in Budapest. Once again, the guards separated them. Olda and Lada together. John by himself. Jarmila with Eva, 11, Vlasta, 6, and Johnny, 2. After two weeks, John was allowed to write to his parents, Joseph and Berta Honolke. His letter, dated October 9, 1948, was brief.

Dear Parents,

Today I am writing you this letter in hopes that you can help me. The situation in Trutnov has forced us to flee on the 15th of September. I had been put in jail for political reasons, so I decided to flee with my family via Kaschau, Hungary and Budapest to Austria.

Our driver was not reliable, so we fell into the hands of the police. We have been in prison 14 days in Szombathelyi, Hungary, and in Budapest. Another trial is waiting us. We have not given up hope and ask you to arrange our immigration permit for us. If this would be possible, we could hopefully become free.

It would be awful to have to return to Czechoslovakia, that would be the end.

But John's letter would not reach his parents in time to save the family. On October 10, authorities transferred John to Törvényszéki Fogház prison in Szombathelyi, to serve a sentence for illegal border crossing.

Guards placed Olda and Lada in another cell for men only. They moved Jarmila—with Eva, Vlasta, and Johnny—to an old brick two-story prison for women and children only. It was nearing winter, November 1948. Jarmila was 27. She sat on a pile of straw with her three children, imprisoned in a strange country.

Helpless and afraid, Jarmila wondered what had happened to the rest of her family. Though she worried about Lada and Olda, she was determined to protect her children. She hoped John was still alive and could find a way to free them. She knew he would never give up. She prayed he would survive his sentence.

The prison was huge, with large, barred windows. Nearly 500 women and children crowded into one large room. Two toilets served the entire population. One was inoperable. Jarmila gathered her young brood around her and fought the growing panic within her.

There were no beds. Just the concrete floor, straw to use as mattresses, and one blanket per family. Bundled in all their clothes and coats, the children huddled close together for warmth. They shivered during the day, constantly rubbing their hands and feet to battle frostbite. Jarmila hoped Olda watched over Lada and prayed they were still alive.

The first night, Eva and Vlasta made a grisly discovery: bed bugs lived in the large cracks of the walls that surrounded them.

When darkness fell, Eva heard them scurrying down the walls and across the concrete floors. She felt the first one crawl across her hand and sat upright, swatting it away.

Vlasta whispered to her sister. "They're attacking us."

"Grab your shoes," Eva said. "We'll kill them so they can't bite Johnny and Mother."

Together, they smacked at the little brown bugs, squashing them by the hundreds. They kept at it until daylight when they saw the red polka dots covered the walls and floor where they had swatted the bugs. Then the two girls fell into a fitful sleep. All around them, mothers and children woke to discover itchy bites on any exposed skin.

This became a routine for the sisters. Every night, thousands of the small, blood-sucking insects poured out of the crevices to feed on the sleeping prisoners. And, every night, Eva and Vlasta stayed awake, cracking the bugs with their shoes to keep them from the one blanket where their mother and Johnny slept.

And so, the days and weeks slid by, with only an occasional scuffle to break the boredom. Twice a day, they filed through the long lines to fill their bowls with a soup made of water, red peppers, and farina as thickener. Sometimes there would be a slice of bread. Jarmila stirred the thin broth and spooned small portions to Johnny.

Each day, the meal was the same. Water thickened with farina, to give it the texture of a thin Cream of Wheat. Salt and pepper for flavoring. And bits of chopped red peppers. Food was scarce everywhere. Prisoners barely survived on two servings a day. Some days, they received two peppers for their meal—one red, one green. Children shrank to skin and bones. Adults lost much of their body weight. All were susceptible to disease.

Once a week, the guards took everyone outside, where they marched single file in a circle around the courtyard. The children longed for the fresh air, but cold winds cut through their thin clothing, making the exercise unbearable.

After a week without bathing, Jarmila was fearful when guards called her name to line up for showers. Struggling to contain her terror, Jarmila followed the nearly silent gathering of prisoners into a stark room with rows of benches. They piled their clothing into neat stacks and entered the shower room, naked. When she heard the hiss of steam begin to flow from the showerheads, Jarmila—and those around her—smashed their children to the floor and covered them with their own bodies, desperately afraid they were inside the gas chambers that had taken the lives of thousands.

When she realized water flowed from the spickets, Jarmila shook the fear from her head. She hurried the children through their showers, helped them dress, and returned to the common area. It was several hours later when her nightmares took control once again, and she lay shivering on their shared blanket with her arms wrapped tightly around young John Jr. She crooned a Czech lullaby.

"Hajej můj andílku hajej a spi, *(Lie my little angel, lie and sleep,)*
matička kolíbá děťátko svý. *(Mum is rocking her baby.)*
Hajej dadej, nynej, malej, *(Lie, sleep sweet, the little one,)*
Matička kolíbá děťátko svý. (Mum is rocking her baby.)*"

Each morning, Jarmila woke with renewed strength. She resolved to endure the cold and the hunger, and hoped John would come for them. By evening, tired and hungry, she relapsed into fear and despair. The longer they waited, the more despondent she became. During her worst days, only Jarmila's fierce love for her children sustained her.

The overcrowded prison was a hotbed of disease. Jarmila was constantly picking fleas and ticks out of John Jr.'s hair. When someone died, the guards dragged them from the common area and the nearby survivors fought over the deceased's blanket. One sultry afternoon, Jarmila heard a heart wrenching wail from a woman sitting with her back to the wall with an infant in her arms. A guard hovered over her. Jarmila watched as the woman clutched her child to her breast until the guard could finally pull the dead baby from her arms. He put the baby's body into a brown paper bag and carried it away.

John Jr. suffered the most from malnutrition those weeks in the prison. The red and green peppers in their daily mush were impossible for him to digest. Although Jarmila constantly scrounged for bits of protein in their porridge to feed her young son, it wasn't enough to keep him healthy. The toddler became seriously ill. Jarmila wrapped him in the blanket, pressed her cool hands to his forehead, and walked the floors to soothe him. When John Jr.'s fever became so high that his little face was scarlet, Jarmila pleaded with a guard for help. The man turned his back and walked away. Later that day, the guard illegally slipped two small aspirins into Jarmila's hands as she filed through the soup line, risking his own life to help her save John Jr. The medicine did its job. John Jr.'s fever broke that night.

Jarmila and her children had survived incarceration for six months. At last, she learned the authorities had tried and convicted her brother, Olda. They sentenced him to life at hard labor and moved him to a Czechoslovakian prison to serve his term. Lada was returned to his mother. Jarmila was happy to have Lada with her, but she had heard nothing from John, and her children were starving.

Then, the unexpected happened. A guard escorted Jarmila and the children to the prison gates and shoved them outside onto a crowded street into the unknown. They were in a foreign city and country, without food or money.

It wasn't until later that they learned John had used the money Jarmila had sewn into his coat to bribe a guard and hire an attorney who negotiated the release for Jarmila and the children. John remained in prison, where they confiscated his coat.

"Now what?" Eva asked her mother.

"I don't know," Jarmila answered.

"But we are alive," Eva said. "Father will find us soon."

"Living without freedom isn't living at all," Jarmila said.

"Where will we go?" Eva was not quite twelve, but she understood her mother's words.

"To Salzburg. Till your father finds us."

"How?"

"I don't know."

"When?"

"I don't know."

The four Honolka children after their release from prison. Back row from left: Lada, Eva, and Vlasta. In front: John Jr.

CHAPTER TWELVE

DP CAMPS

They trudged their way along the crowded streets to the railroad depot and boarded a train. Two ticket collectors approached them as the train was about to pull out of the station. Jarmila had no tickets and pleaded with them.

"In the name of God and these little children, don't send me back."

The older man exchanged a glance with the younger one. "I don't see anything. Do you?"

"No, sir."

The weary family stayed on the train all the way to Vienna.

Exhausted and hungry, Jarmila approached strangers for directions to the nearest shelter. They walked several miles before they reached the refugee camp. Jarmila left the younger children in Eva's care while she searched for other Czech refugees who could answer her questions.

She spoke with an older woman in the food line.

"We are Czech, and we've just come from prison in Hungary. Will my children be safe here?"

"Not if you are fleeing the Russians," the woman said. "Vienna is still in a Russian zone. If they discover you are here, the Soviet authorities will send you back to Czechoslovakia."

"Please. Nemůžeme se vrátit," Jarmila said. "We can't go back."

"Then find your way to the displaced persons camp in Salzburg. It is in the French zone."

Before dawn on their second day in Vienna, Jarmila hurried her children out of the camp and onto the dusty road, where they again slipped into the crowds, unnoticed. Without road signs to guide them, the little family walked quickly in the direction most people appeared to be headed. They had gone several miles before Jarmila heard a woman speaking Czech to her companion. She called out to her.

"Excuse me. Can you tell me how far it is to Salzburg?"

"It's far," she answered. "Nearly 300 kilometers. But you must turn around. There is a Russian camp ahead. Go back the way you have come and take the fork to the right."

Jarmila and her children crossed the street and began the journey in the opposite direction. They walked at a steady pace, passing by elderly refugees, too frail to walk. Old men and women sat in ditches begging for food and water. But Jarmila had nothing to give them. She and Eva took turns hoisting Johnny onto their backs, when his short legs could walk no further.

After the fork in the road, a farmer hauling a load of hay pulled over to offer them a ride. In the middle of a center pile of hay, the farmer had created a space large enough to hide a family. They scrambled onto the wagon and waited for the farmer to cover them with the hay. The three younger children quickly fell asleep as the wagon rattled over the country roads. An hour into the journey, the farmer pulled to a stop. Jarmila and Eva heard raised voices as the farmer argued with the people who had forced him off the road.

"I'm a simple farmer, delivering hay," the farmer said.

"No one passes the checkpoint without our permission," a Russian guard said.

"But I am returning to Salzburg. I have my papers,"

"Then you will not mind if we check your load," the Russian answered.

Jarmila and Eva held their breath as the Russians shoved pitchforks into the hay around them. One fork landed so close to Eva's head that she could touch the metal prong above her,

Finding nothing but hay, the guards allowed the farmer to pass, and the kind man drove them all the way to a displaced persons camp in Salzburg.

The Honolkas were not alone in their desire to flee the country. Millions of displaced people poured across the borders seeking asylum. The need was so great that the UN General Assembly created the International Refugee Organization (IRO) to take over all responsibilities for a network of camps offering housing, food and medical care, as well as assisting with resettlement. After two years of delays, the IRO finally launched on August 20, 1948, the same year John and his family were out of prison.[xxv]

The IRO embarked on a comprehensive large-scale program and worldwide operational field activities. Eighteen member governments underwrote their efforts. (Including the US which contributed nearly half of the $430 million the organization would spend in the next three years.) The IRO's goal was to arrange for the rehabilitation and retraining of refugees, as well as for their legal protection. In addition, it negotiated agreements for resettlement, brought the refugees to ports of embarkation, and, in a vast shipping operation, transported them overseas. The assignment was all encompassing, and nearly impossible to fulfill.

While the IRO assumed primary responsibility for the displaced persons in Europe, they only operated camps in the American Zones of Austria and Germany. The British and French operated their own zones, in collaboration with the IRO. The camps differed in their language, governmental structure, and local requirements; but all provided shelter, food, clothing and medical care for the refugees.

From the beginning, overcrowding was inevitable in the Displaced Persons (DP) Camps. Families clung to each other and did their best to survive. Most suffered from disease and malnutrition. Jarmila and her four children were assigned a room in the barracks of the Salzburg Displaced Persons Camp. For the first time since they had fled their home nearly eight months earlier, they were together in their own private space. The journey had taken them from Czechoslovakia to the prison in Hungary, to the DP Camp in Vienna, and finally to Salzburg. Jarmila was exhausted, but hopeful that she could somehow find her husband here.

For the first several days, Jarmila worked to navigate her way through the system. The administrators at the Austrian camp spoke primarily German, with a Bavarian dialect. American Red Cross teams spoke English. Jarmila spoke German. She gave them John's name and the prison where he had been sentenced. They promised to alert her if they found him.

Most of the families sheltering in the DP Camps referred to them as "lagers" or "lager camps." The facilities consisted of long wooden barracks, divided into larger rooms—one for each family. For a little privacy, the family attached a rope from one side of the room to the other, hanging a blanket over the rope to serve as a dividing wall. A separate barrack building served as a restroom, with six to eight holes and no division between them. Each week, someone splashed the latrines with bleach.

The food in the lager was not much better than what the prison had served. Every day, Jarmila and the children stood in line, waiting their turn with shallow metal plates—like those used for panning gold—to receive a ladle-full of the kitchen's offerings.

Vlasta seemed the most content in the Salzburg DP Camp. She wanted to draw or paint, but she had no crayons. Since the children had nothing but a dirt yard, the little girl improvised. After it rained, the seven-year-old gathered different hues of mud and clay, mixed them with water and painted pictures on the ground. Sometimes she found bits of broken pottery or dishes to play with; she kept herself occupied for hours.

It was a sunny day in late summer when Jarmila caught a glimpse of a man across the crowded outdoor gathering space. She noticed the set of his shoulders. His stride. She stared at him until his face came into full view. Then, she handed John Jr. to his big sister Eva and raced through the masses of people to run into her husband's arms. John Honolka had again bribed prison guards and hired an Austrian attorney with the money Jarmila had sewn into his coat lining. It had taken the attorney less than a month to obtain John's release from prison on November 9, 1948. It had taken another six months for the Red Cross to locate John's family.

Jarmila led John to where their children stood. He bent to hug them, but they didn't recognize this skinny stranger with hollow cheeks, ragged clothes, and tangled hair. They backed away from him in fear. It wasn't until they heard his voice, speaking softly to them, when they realized he was their father. Johnny barely remembered him.

Tuttlingen DP Camp

Soon after John's arrival in Salzburg the spring of 1949, the family fled to another Lager Camp in Tuttlingen, Germany. Because Austria had remained neutral during the Cold War following World War II, authorities often detained refugees who flooded across its borders. New camps were opening across Germany, and John hoped for better conditions there. When they reached Tuttlingen Lager, they discovered it was like all the others—with long wooden barracks and overcrowded rooms. Unfortunately, it was also infested with rats. The family could hear them running in the attic overhead at night, and see them outside, looking for food.

John chose not to mention the rat infestation when he wrote to his mother about the new camp. Instead, he used glowing descriptions that embellished the truth. In reality, Tuttlingen was located on the Danube River, but the swimming pool did not exist.

John wrote:

"Everything was ready for us. We have two rooms; we are well taken care of. The camp includes more than Czech refugees—mostly Polish, Ukrainian and Hungarian people are here. Five minutes from camp is a swimming pool, and the city is surrounded by mountains and forests. The town is as big as Trutnov, and the Danube River flows through it."

With his business background and leadership skills, John became the camp's leader. Another Czech, 22-year-old law student, Frantisek Neuman (later changed to Frank Newman), was leader of a different lager. The two

men met in the camps, where the French secret police recruited each of
them to help screen newcomers: interviewing new arrivals to determine
whether they were Communist spies or actual political refugees. Although
John was sixteen years older than Frank, it wasn't long before they developed
a close friendship.

"Tell me your story," John said to the younger man.

"There's not much to tell, sir," Frank responded. "When I was 16, I
enrolled in Karl University in Prague. I thought I wanted to be a
Catholic priest."

John grinned at the young man. "Change of plans?"

Frank shrugged his shoulders. "The education broadened my horizons. I
studied languages, philosophy, and law."

"You speak English?"

Frank counted on his fingers as he recited: "English, Latin, German,
French, Russian, and Polish."

"And Czechoslovakian," John added. "Seven languages?"

"Once I got started, it was hard to stop."

"You had a good education."

"Yes. We read the great philosophers—Plato, Socrates and Karl Marx.
That's what spurred my interest in the law."

Another evening, John and Frank sat by a campfire outside the barrack-
style housing. They studied the stars and talked of their plans to live
in freedom again. John spoke about his thriving factory and how the
Communists had taken it from him.

"After the war ended, I had high hopes for our country. But the
Communists who controlled our government were like the Nazis."

Frank described his own journey. "I was in a college preparatory program
in Prague but was forced into a Nazi slave labor group in 1945. After the war,
I was accepted into Charles University as a law student."

"Yet you are here," John said.

"I have the Communists to thank for that, Mr. Honolka. I joined with some other students in protest when the Soviets took over our country. That was enough to get me expelled from Czechoslovakia."

"Were you imprisoned?"

"I fled the secret police in 1948 but was captured in '49. Then, I escaped again and made my way to Vienna and finally to French-occupied Germany, where I ended up in Bad Wurzbach Lager. Today, I am here with you."

The two had much in common. Forced from their homeland, both had fought for freedom. Both were well educated. Both sought asylum in Norway, the USA, or New Zealand. Eva, now eleven, often sat near her father to listen to them talk. All she remembered of her life was the fear that soldiers would kill her family. The conversations between her father and his new friend were always about freedom. When they dreamed of what life could be in a new land, Eva could close her eyes and picture a better world.

Frank barely noticed the frail little girl who often lingered near her father. He was too busy helping the hundreds of displaced persons who found their way to him for advice on their paperwork. Fluent in seven languages, he was in high demand for translations and legal assistance, even though he had not completed law school.

Because he talked to so many people, Frank always seemed to hear about new developments before anyone else. He was on a first-name basis with many of the Red Cross workers and often traveled between lagers to help families find their loved ones. One day, he returned from a trip and rushed to locate John where he stood in the long line, waiting for the evening meal.

Frank greeted his friend then leaned toward him. "Can we talk tonight? I may have found a way to America!"

"I'll meet you at our usual spot," John said.

The sun hung low in the sky as the two men sat across from each other. John saw the excitement in Frank's eyes. "You are bursting with news," he said. "Do you have a sponsor who will get you to America?"

"Yes. The U.S. Army!"

"You're enlisting as a foreign citizen?"

"If they will have me," Frank said. "It's a fast track to citizenship."

"But you could be sent into battle anywhere in the world," John said.

"At least I will be fighting for freedom." Frank's eyes shone with passion. "I can make a difference for others."

John watched the young man's progress with interest. "Mark my words, Jarmila. That boy has a bright future ahead of him."

Even when assigned to different lagers, he and John stayed in touch. Both men pushed forward with their efforts to immigrate—John through the American Red Cross, and Frank through the U.S. Army. Although their hopes were high, the process was slow.

CHAPTER THIRTEEN

THE CHILDREN ARE STARVING

In April of 1949, twelve countries—Belgium, France, Luxembourg, the Netherlands, the United Kingdom, Canada, Denmark, Iceland, Italy, Norway, Portugal, and the United States—signed an agreement in Washington DC, creating a formal alliance called the North Atlantic Treaty Organization (NATO). The treaty committed each member state to consider any armed attack against another member state, in Europe or North America, to be an attack against them all.

John read about NATO in the camp newspaper. He considered it progress, but it had no immediate impact on their family. He and Jarmila struggled to feed and clothe their children. Vlasta had outgrown her shoes. She went barefoot while they hoped for a Red Cross shipment that might contain shoes to fit her. Most contained food only. The camp received separate clothing shipments, bur children's clothing and shoe supplies were meager.

They had cheap metal plates, bowls, and cups that gave a metallic taste to all the food served on them. Nothing tasted right. When the care packages came, they included powdered eggs, Carnation condensed milk, or two-pound boxes of whole milk powder. Sometimes, the boxes included one- or two-pound tins of margarine, lard, peanut butter, chocolate, and a dab of coffee. Occasionally, there was oatmeal or Cream of Wheat. Every package was a source of joy—in part because it was a change from daily events—but more so for the extra food they supplied. John favored the small tins of sardines, but Vlasta hated them.

The population in the DP Camps multiplied so quickly the food rations could not keep up with the demand. John and Jarmila gave most of their portions to the children, but it wasn't enough. Refugees caught rats and mice, which they cooked and ate to survive. Dogs and cats were disappearing, also. Eva, Lada, and Vlasta lost weight. Their ribs showed through their skin and dark circles formed under their eyes.

Jarmila and John could no longer watch their children starve.

"We have to do something," Jarmila said.

"I'll talk to the Red Cross. We'll see what they can do."

John returned from his meeting with a spring in his step. "We have an opportunity," he told Jarmila. "But we must let our children go to Switzerland without us. Families there have offered temporary homes for school-age refugees."

Jarmila reluctantly agreed.

The summer of 1949, they applied through the Red Cross for host families to take Eva, Lada and Vlasta. Then they waited for a response. Jarmila hoped to place the three children together, but no one had space for all three. Several families expressed an interest in Lada. Fewer wanted to sponsor girls. Now, John spent his days filling out paperwork for school applications and visas, in addition to the documents required for their emigration from Europe.

Lindau DP Camp

Their latest "home" in the lager at Lindau, Germany, consisted of two rooms and included two wooden bunk beds. Only one bed had a mattress. Since Vlasta was the shortest of the three older children, she slept on a faded red wooden crate next to the window until they could find a mattress, or another suitable replacement. Without the mattress, the child was small enough to fall out of the bunk bed between the wooden planks.

In the middle of June, John sent his sister, Helene, a letter from their DP Camp in Lindau, Germany, describing his frustration.

June 14, 1949

Dear Sister,

We received your last letter. On the 3rd and 4th, we were in Tuttlingen, Germany, to get shots. Now Honzik (John Jr.) has a high fever and has lost weight. Also, we moved to a different barracks. We have a larger room. It is easier.

I received a letter from New York City regarding our moving to the United States of America. If things do not work out with Norway, I will stay here for a while, then immigrate to the United States of America.

Last week I was in Ludwigshafen, Stuttgart, Ulm, and Friedrichshafen, Germany. Got a lot accomplished. I am going to wait 14 days, then I will let you know about vacation. The weather is better now, but we have had a lot of rain. The water in the lake is warm, it is great for swimming; the children have a nice tan. Honzik (Johnny) tells everyone that Helene has gone in a large railroad car.

We have not heard anything from Trutnov. We received the package from Mother. It had a head pillow for Honzik. Lada received an invitation from Switzerland again. Also, he got a package with chocolate and condensed milk.

It is okay here, but I wish I had something to do. I also received a card from H. Prelat. He does not seem to realize what goes on in the world. Everything is probably going to come to a head by next year, but not much is known or written about it.

You can all hope to get back home, just wait and see. Should we suddenly go, I will write right away, so you know. All the best from all of us, also Honzik (John Jr)

Hans

Jarmila read the letter before John mailed it. "You make things sound better than they are," she said. "In truth, the children are still starving. They are not tan and healthy."

"I don't want them to worry," John said. "It is better to stress the positive."

"Do you really believe we will be able to go home again?"

"I don't know. But they can hope. If the government changes again in a few years, it could happen. With the NATO Alliance in place, it should be difficult for any single country to start a war against another."

Later that month, John wrote to his mother from the Lindau lager.

June 30, 1949

Dear Mom,

I received your card. I was convinced that I had written to you, meanwhile I wrote to Willie. The package arrived in good condition, and Honzik received his pillow. He does remember grandmother well. We were pleased about the shoes from father and your delicious cake.

The children are outside in fresh air all day, and in the afternoon they are by the lake, and eat three times as much as they did at home. Today I could use my stockpile that I left at home. Now they also must eat dry bread. Everyone is tanned and Honzik has also recovered. We were in Tuttlingen, Germany, four weeks ago for a medical examination where he received shots. A week later, he got a high fever and was bedridden for three days.

Monday Helene will come to us and spend her vacation here for 24 days. Hopefully, everything will go well and we do not have to leave suddenly.

We are very curious where we will end up. From Stuttgart, Germany, we will travel by airplane to Oslo, Norway. Already received a message from them that they are preparing everything for us. Altogether, a total of 152 Czechs are accepted by Norway from all camps. 45 from Lindau, Germany, and the first six are already gone. Twelve will be returned to the CSR (Czech Socialist Republic) as partisans. They will be well equipped and paid. However, if they get caught, they will hang. Surely you are following the events in the CSR in "Die Neu Zeitung" (The New Newspaper). It will all be short lived. Everything will be over in 1951.

We have received a message from Milek Kralik (Jarmila's older brother) that he is still doing some business, but it is very weak. In Trutnov there is an exhibit in the converted Faltis factory—linen manufacturer and a cotton weaving mill.

Oldrich (Olda) Kralik was sentenced to two years in prison for simply trying to cross the border. We did not know that he was already in Salzburg, Germany. He is in Trutnov. Couldn't you come to us next Sunday with the discounted return ticket? It is a good connection with an express train. The train arrives at half past eleven in Lindau, and you could go back Monday morning. Inform yourself, and if possible, come.

That same day, June 30, 1949, Jarmila wrote to her in-laws (John's parents).

June 30, 1949

Dear Grandmother and Grandfather,

First, I want to thank you for all the good things you have sent us. It is always well received. Often, your shipments have helped us in our bad situation. Maybe, later, we will have a chance to pay you back for everything.

Please, everyone stay healthy so that we can all meet happily in Trutnov. If you can, please come and visit us. It would make us all happy—especially, it would make the children happy.

Eva often asks about you and Deda (Grandfather). Also, Lada and Vlasta think of you and talk about how nice it was when we all lived together in Trutnov. Next week, Helene is coming to us. Please, if you can, come also. Before we leave, I will write another letter.

Honzik (John Senior) and the children go swimming at Bodensee (Lake Constance). John Jr. speaks German very well but mixes Czech with it, which is a lot of fun.

Warm greetings to you both.

Your Jarmila

Except for their daily struggle to feed their family, July and August 1949 were happier months for Jarmila. She was grateful to have John by her side, and her children close. The lager wasn't easy, but it was far better than the prison had been. Here, Jarmila and John could work toward their dream of relocating their family to a free country. John's optimism always lifted her spirits.

During the late summer and early fall, John and Vlasta would walk along the railroad tracks for miles, collecting coal that had fallen from the coal car. They saved it in the red wooden crate to use in the stove when winter came.

One day in early September, Jarmila woke up with a queasy stomach. Since illnesses quickly spread through the crowded camp, and medical care was limited, Jarmila could not see a doctor. She had no fever, but she fainted after breakfast. That afternoon, Jarmila rested on the mattress in their barracks while Eva held a cold cloth on her forehead. After three days, Jarmila felt stronger. She went to John with the news.

"I'm not sick, John. I'm pregnant."

"This is good," John said. "Maybe our child will be born free."

"All our children were born free, but freedom was stolen from them," Jarmila said.

By the fall of 1949, Vlasta still had no shoes. She had run barefoot since the spring. Now, the frost had arrived. Jarmila found an old cardboard box and called out to Vlasta.

"Come. I will make a pair of shoes for you," she said.

Jarmila flattened the box into a sheet and directed Vlasta to stand on it. She traced the outline of her daughter's feet, then cut the cardboard along the outline with a knife. Lada had also outgrown his brown corduroy jacket. Jarmila cut the back of the jacket out, split the fabric in half, and placed the cardboard cutout in the center of each half. She used her one remaining needle and the last of her thread to sew the corduroy and cardboard together, struggling to force the needle through the thick cardboard. She formed a flap, made a buttonhole, and used the button from the front of the jacket to close the flap.

The shoes looked more like slippers, but Vlasta didn't care.

"They are not beautiful," her mother said, "but they will keep your feet warm for a little while."

Wearing her cardboard slippers, Vlasta walked through the woods to attend a local school. There, the older German boys laughed at her homemade shoes; they chased her and stomped on her feet with their heavy boots. Vlasta ignored them. Holding her head high, she refused to cry. The young girl had learned an important lesson during the time she spent in prison with her mother and siblings: never show fear or pain, even when you are afraid or hurting.

The wheels of bureaucracy moved far too slowly, and their family was still stuck in a Lager watching others leave for "resettlement centers" every day. Sponsors were unwilling to take the responsibility for a larger family. Small families were always chosen first.

The displaced persons population had declined to around 600,000 people—half in the camps, and the remainder in communities or on farms. These "out-of-camp refugees" still had no homes but wanted to stay in Europe. Others, like the Honolkas who hoped to emigrate from their homelands, would advance from the camps into short-term resettlement centers in Germany and Austria as their paperwork progressed.

The American immigration authorities required a two-year investigation into the background of every refugee—researching medical histories as far back as the grandparents. If a grandfather had tuberculosis, for example, they refused the family for fear someone might carry the disease.

After they received their visas from the consular officials at the resettlement center, they would move to an embarkation center for a final clearance by immigration officials before sailing. Jarmila feared the size of their family was one reason the process was taking so long. They were still at least two moves away from their elusive dream of boarding a ship to freedom.

CHAPTER FOURTEEN

THE FAMILY GROWS

Winters were brutal in Eastern Europe. The lager's bedroom was ice cold. The wooden building had no insulation, and the wood was thin. Concerned that his children might freeze, John trekked into the forest and illegally cut down a tree to chop into wood for the family's stove. He and Vlasta carried it to the lager in homemade backpacks, where they stored it in the only piece of furniture they owned—the multipurpose faded red wooden crate.

The thin scratchy woolen blankets were as cold as the bedroom. The children would crawl under them and cover their heads for a long time before their body heat warmed them. Through John's ingenuity, they found a way to maximize the heat from their small stove. He found four bricks and heated them on top of the small potbelly stove in the main room. When they were hot, he wrapped each brick in a piece of cloth and placed them at the foot of the bunk beds. The bricks heated the beds and stayed warm for hours. When the brick cooled a little, the children placed their feet on the warm brick and fell asleep.

By that December, Jarmila was six months pregnant. With her poor diet in the Lager Camp, she gained no weight. Because they were not German citizens, they had no access to public health care or other services, so she did her best to monitor her own pregnancy. The camp doctor was busy caring for the sick or dying. He had no time for a healthy pregnant woman.

The paperwork for their three older children to spend a school semester in Switzerland had still not come through. Jarmila and John worried they might suffer long-term consequences from malnutrition.

At last, a few days before Christmas, Lada's papers arrived. John wrote to his parents with the news.

December 28, 1949

Dear Parents,

On Tuesday, the 27th of December, we received a nice Christmas package from Willie. (John's brother) Lada also received a package from his foster parents in Switzerland. He got a nice sweater, chocolate, four games, Nescafe and cookies, candies, dates, and figs.

On the 23rd of December, I received papers from the French for Lada to move to Switzerland. We waited for two months. Now, Lada can go at the end of January for three months to Rapperswil, Switzerland. I also got a visa for Switzerland. On the 27th, I went with Lada to the French police in Lindau to get the papers. It cost 33 DM (Deutsche Marks) for the passport. Helene's Christmas check went towards this.

We had a nice Christmas and are satisfied. But, without your help, it would not be that way. We had a small tree and bought school supplies for the kids. Honzik (John Jr) got a wooden train. Vlasta got coloring books and colored pencils. The best gift was from Helene. The money was very appreciated.

On Sunday, we had a gift giving for the children in the camp. There was a large tree with electric lights in the mess hall. Each child received a sack filled with nuts, figs, dates, chocolates, mandarin oranges, cookies and a few other things. Honzik and Vlasta also received a small metal wagon. Eva got bacon, meat fat, and milk.

On Christmas, we had potato salad and sausages. Two pigs were slaughtered in camp. We had pork both holidays. We were also photographed. Jarmila looked sad; she was probably homesick.

Eva has a lot of friends here. She goes to school with them. There was singing for the Christmas program.

I'll let you know in the New Year, if I can get to Norway.

Mr. Beier sent a package with pfeffernusse cookies and wafers. We were happy about that. We have not yet received the clothes we were promised.

In truth, the coloring book Vasta received consisted of two pages and four colored pencils. The sack of goodies included only two walnuts, one mandarin orange, and eight pieces of hard Christmas candy—no figs, dates, chocolates, or cookies. (Though the children were happy to receive the sweets in the bag.) There was no metal wagon. Eva didn't get bacon, meat, or milk. There was no potato salad or sausage. And no pig slaughter in the lager. John exaggerated by incorporating his happy memories of past Christmases, when the family enjoyed potato salad and salami on Christmas Eve.

The letter would be the last one John wrote to his father, Joseph.

Early in 1950, John received word that Joseph, 82, had suffered a stroke. John and Eva traveled home to be with him. He and his mother, Berta Marie, 59, sat beside Joseph's hospital bed, reminiscing about the good times they had shared.

John remembered his father, the railroad conductor, as a hero for preventing a collision between two trains when he was a young man. His father was the biggest, strongest man John knew. His voice had been powerful, then. Not loud, but forceful. When his father spoke, John obeyed. Now he could not speak at all.

March 13 began like any other day in the lager. The family stood in line with their metal plates for a helping of breakfast porridge. Jarmila took Johnny outside to the play yard, and John walked to the post office. Jarmila felt the twinge of a light labor pain in her abdomen just after lunch. By mid-afternoon, the pains were stronger and more frequent.

Jarmila laid her hand on John's arm.

"We should request a car," she said. "The baby's coming."

John rushed to the camp office. "It's my wife," he said. "She's having a baby."

Jarmila made the trip to the local convent. She gazed out the car window on the way. The driver took the most direct route, around the beautiful lake where John took the kids swimming, over the medieval stone bridge, into the picturesque village, and past the local hospital where refugees were not allowed inside. The nuns who welcomed her surveyed the petite woman with concern.

Not surprisingly, the baby was born frail and small. Jarmila held him in her arms and crooned to him.

"Your name is Thomas Jaromir Honolka," she told him. "And I am your mother."

While Jarmila was at the convent, regaining her strength, John negotiated with the camp directors for additional space. The family acquired another room in the barracks. John did the laundry while Jarmila was away, boiling all the clothes outside in a large kettle. He tossed everything into the wash, not sorting by colors. One bright red piece of clothing turned all the white underwear pink. When she returned to the camp with their newborn son, Jarmila stood in the new room and admired John's work, overwhelmed by all the pink.

The children oohed and ahhed over their baby brother. Soon, their search for food centered on the baby's needs. Everyone looked for the fruits and vegetables that were scarce in the camp.

Jarmila fed Thomas like a baby bird. The older children sacrificed anything from their own rations that could be cooked, pureed, mashed or smashed; the baby's needs were a priority. When Eva traded a schoolmate a pencil for an apple, Jarmila scraped the fruit with a spoon to make a sauce for Thomas.

If an occasional cup of Cream of Wheat became available, they reserved it for the baby. The family had a new mission: to love and protect their tiny brother.

They had barely welcomed the new baby into their family when Jarmila had to say goodbye to her oldest son. On Sunday, March 27, when Thomas was not quite two weeks old, John and John Jr. took Lada to meet his Swiss sponsor family.

The camp driver dropped them off at the dock in Konstanz, Germany, where they boarded a ship for the four-hour ride to Kreuzlingen, Switzerland. Three-year-old John Jr. held tight to his father's hand as the boat left the dock. Lada, 10, raised his face to the sun while the cool breeze from the Rhine River ruffled his hair.

John studied Lada's face. "How do you feel, son?"

"Happy and scared," Lada said.

"That's the sign of a good adventure ahead."

"It's my first time away from home."

"You are a smart boy. And brave," John said. "Just do your best. No one can expect more."

"I will, Father."

"We want you to come back to us, happy and healthy."

The Customs Office at the border town moved quickly through Lada's paperwork. John shook hands with Oswald and Berta Wanner, Lada's foster parents.

"Thank you for welcoming Lada into your home," he said.

"Don't worry. We will take good care of him," Berta said.

"We will drive through Winterhur, then Zurich, before we arrive at Rapperswil, St. Gallen," Oswald said. "It will take less than two hours, so I imagine we will be home before you are back in Konstanz."

John and Johnny stood at the dock and waved goodbye as the Swiss couple drove away with Lada. The last image John saw was his son's thin face pressed against the glass of the car window.

CHAPTER FIFTEEN

PUSHING FORWARD

For the next several weeks, John spent as much time seeking temporary placements for Eva and Vlasta as researching options for the family's long-term emigration. Soon, someone invited Eva to visit the canton of Graubunden, Switzerland, located even deeper into the Swiss Alps.

John and Jarmila studied the new application together.

"Eva would probably do well there," Jarmila said.

"It's an hour or two farther from us than Lada," John said.

Jarmila rubbed her temples. "We have to find the money for the visa."

They didn't have to wait long. On May 12, two days before her 13th birthday, Eva's chance arrived. John received a letter from his mother. She enclosed 20 DM (Deutsche Marks), enough to help fund Eva's Swiss visa and travel pass, which totaled 37 DMs. John carried it directly to the German police. They scheduled Eva's departure date for July 2.

Lada's host family wrote a glowing letter requesting that he remain with them all summer. Lada sent a postcard from Lucerne. Their son had already experienced a school ski trip to the Alps, where he learned to race down the slopes with his classmates. Now, his hosts were showing him more of their country.

While they waited for Eva's trip, John taught Eva and Vlasta to swim in Lake Constance at Lindau. John Jr. (Honzik) joined them in the warm water, splashing about for several hours each day. Jarmila brought Thomas along for the sunshine. The baby was good natured from the beginning, smiling for everyone he met.

On July 2, Eva traveled to Switzerland alone. She boarded the boat and set off to meet her host parents. Jarmila missed both her children desperately, but she was determined to have them back, and healthy, before the family emigrated from Europe. John and Jarmila remained at the Lindau Displaced Persons Camp with Vlasta, Johnny, and Thomas. Eva and Lada stayed with their host families in Switzerland. They attended school and waited for news of their pending trip to another country, another unknown.

In early September, the food arrangements changed at the DP Camp. The communal kitchen closed, and each family received their own kitchen stove, as well as food vouchers to use at local merchants. The coupons allowed them quantities of meat, vegetables, bread and butter to last ten days. They could do their own shopping and prepare their own meals—but needed to track their purchases. Jarmila welcomed the change. She had become used to stretching food rations to feed her family. This would give her more control over their meals.

The two older children thrived with their host families. Eva made new friends in Switzerland and adapted quickly to her school. She wrote letters about the food. Lada excelled at sports. He was polite, helped around the house, and applied himself to learning English.

In mid-September, Eva and Lada arrived at the Lindau camp for a visit. Eva had gained 10 kg. (22 pounds), and Lada 4 kg (8.8 pounds). Jarmila was overjoyed to see them. Arrangements had finally come together for Vlasta to stay with a host couple in Switzerland, and they hoped she would also gain weight. When all three of their older children were safely off to Switzerland, John and Jarmila breathed a sigh of relief. They felt certain the emigration process would move forward soon, and they could reunite their family for the move to America.

Each week, they received encouraging reports from both Eva and Lada's host families, but Vlasta's hosts, a lovely middle-aged couple, expressed concerns. Vlasta was shy in school. She had not made friends and struggled with her classes. When she had not improved after several weeks, they wrote to Jarmila and John.

"We worry about Vlasta's health," they said. "She seems homesick and has no appetite. We wonder if she would be happier in a family with children. Would you agree to a transfer?"

John and Jarmila approved the transfer and Vlasta moved into a different host family. The couple had two children of their own. But the new family and school made things worse, instead of better. Eight-year-old Vlasta was smaller than her classmates. She missed her own family. When John and Jarmila learned how unhappy Vlasta was, they arranged for her to return to the camp.

In 1950, there were still an estimated 1,250,000 or more refugees throughout the world. Of these, the International Refugee Organization (IRO) had registered 400,000, but had not yet settled them into new locations; instead, they remained in Germany and Austria, with an unknown but substantial number of unregistered out-of-camp refugees. In addition, new refugees from the countries of Eastern Europe continued to flow into Western Europe.

Norway was John's first choice for his family, but he was also a realist. After months of waiting for an American sponsor, he applied to Australia and New Zealand, as well. One afternoon, he handed Jarmila a newspaper with an advertisement circled in red.

"What would you think of moving to Quito, Ecuador?"

Jarmila studied the ad. "Why not? You have all the qualifications they want. And the weather in Central America would be warmer."

"We might have to learn Spanish. But we would live in a furnished villa and be paid 3,000 Cruzeiro per month."

Jarmila burst into laughter. "I have no idea what that means. Do you?"

He shrugged his shoulders. "It is more than I make now."

"Send your letter," Jarmila said. "We can dream of our new home in the Spanish villa."

"Don't pack your bags too soon," John replied. "They speak Spanish, and my letter is written in English."

After the arrival of their precious new baby, Jarmila had settled into their lives at the German refugee camp, determined to make the best of it. She had hoped and prayed for nearly eight years—through all of World War II, then the Communist Russia takeover, and the years of imprisonment and detention. Although she tried to hide it, Jarmila was homesick and discouraged. If not for John's unwavering faith, she would have given up long ago.

No matter what obstacles they faced, John refused to let go of the dream. When he spoke of freedom, his eyes shone with hope. Jarmila and the children sat in a circle around him. They listened as he described their new home and the adventures they would share.

He talked of freedom, his vision of their new home, and his expectations for the children to go to school in a free world. He believed their own country would return to freedom within a few years, so they could all return to their beloved mountains, their home. When John described their new house, Jarmila always said she hoped there would be large windows. She loved the sun.

Life in the lager was a constant challenge. All displaced persons had experienced trauma, and many had serious health conditions because of what they had endured. The camps had been established to provide shelter, nutrition and basic health care, but John and Jarmila knew first-hand that the camp food was far from nutritious. Medical care was minimal. Displaced persons often moved from camp to camp, looking for family, countrymen, freedom, or better food and accommodation. Over time, ethnic and religious groups concentrated in certain camps.

With the steady flow of people moving in and out, and inadequate diets of less than 800 - 1,000 calories a day, new diseases broke out every week. People were often filthy, lice-ridden, and exhausted. The refugees watched as the most vulnerable among them—infants and the elderly—succumbed to the unsanitary conditions. Every week, more people died in the camps. One winter, the Honolka family survived by supplementing their diet with apples from an orchard on the outskirts of the lager and from trees in nearby yards. They were allowed to take apples that had fallen to the ground, so the children gathered what they found and stored them in the versatile red wooden crate in their room. The temperature was cool enough that the fruit didn't rot.

Beyond the critical need for food and medicines, the sheer numbers of refugees in the camps created multiple problems. Clothing was in short supply. Space was limited. Finding a moment of privacy was nearly impossible. Many of the refugees suffered from psychological difficulties. They were distrustful, apprehensive, depressed, and traumatized. The environment was ripe for crime.

Still, the camps managed to offer some educational and cultural activities. People celebrated holidays, married, gave birth, held church services, and wrote to their loved ones. They spent many hours completing mountains of paperwork and navigating through laws and regulations to apply for immigration into countries that would accept them.

Despite all their setbacks, John remained obsessed with the hope of immigrating into a different country, like Norway, to freedom and opportunity. He talked about it. He dreamed about it often, and he prayed for it to happen.

Jarmila became increasingly discouraged and heartsick. She missed her family more each day. In search of freedom, she and John left behind their home, friends, parents, and roots; they took only their children and the clothes on their backs. She wondered if they would ever be free again. She prayed that John would not lose heart if his efforts failed.

CHAPTER SIXTEEN

GOING TO AMERICA

The letter arrived when they least expected it. An American sponsor—a farmer and his wife—had agreed to support their entire family. He sent a few photographs documenting his property: four farms, 12,000 acres of land, 150 cattle, six horses, three tractors and modern equipment. He was 78. He wrote he had reserved a house for the Honolka family on one of his farms.

The good news did not speed the American immigration process. When John still didn't have a US departure plan by the end of September, he went to the Australian Commission.

In the fall of 1950, Jarmila received another letter from Lada's foster family. She tore it open, eager to learn of her son's latest accomplishments. Instead, she read an unexpected offer:

Dear Jarmila and John,

We have come to love your son, Lada, as our own. He is a wonderful boy— bright and athletic, good-natured and fun-loving. He is doing well in school and has many friends. He has become an expert at snow skiing. As you have seen from his visits, Lada has gained weight and become healthy again. He has his own room, but also enjoys spending time with us, as we take him to see the sights of Switzerland.

Today we write to say we would like to adopt Lada and raise him here, with our family. We have the resources to provide him with a good home, education, and future. Of course, we would encourage him to stay in touch with you through letters and visits. Please consider this so we can discuss arrangements.

Very truly yours,
Oswald and Berta Wanner

Lada's Swiss Family

Jarmila's eyes filled with tears. Her hands shook as she handed the letter to John. "We have already lost too much," she said. "We cannot lose our son. Bring him home. Now."

Eva and Lada both returned from their foster homes in Switzerland, rejoining their family to prepare for the long-awaited trip to America. John wrote to his mother about the good news.

"Lada and Eva both look exceptionally good. Eva has gained 10 kg, and Lada 4 kg."

That September, John reassured his family that they would soon live near the kind landowner in the United States. Although they still had applications out to Australia, the American paperwork appeared to be moving faster.

Two months later, in late November, the plans were nearly complete. The family was called to Rastatt, Germany, to be checked by an American doctor, and then to the local consulate to apply for their visas.

On Nov. 23, 1950, when John wrote to share the news with his mother, he was uncertain whether the family would go to America or Australia. He was hopeful, but not ready to trust that the March 12 journey to Bremen, Germany, would take place on schedule.

If all went well, Bremen would be their final stay before they went to Bremerhaven Port (where the Elbe River fed into the North Sea, across from the United Kingdom coastline). There, they would board a ship to cross the ocean.

John told his mother of their tentative plans:

"Friday morning at 11 a.m., we were introduced to the Consul of Bremen, who granted us the entry permit. We will be transported from Rastatt to Bremen, Germany, on the 12th of March."

"We have already been documented, photographed, and fingerprinted. If all goes well, we can finally leave in April or May—but that is not certain, because just last week I was notified by the IRO that I could go to New Zealand...

The family made plans for a March trip to Bremen, to await the overseas journey. However, on Thursday, Dec. 14, 1950, only a few weeks after they returned from Rastatt to Lindau, John received an urgent notice from the Lindau DP Camp administrator. Instead of waiting until March 12, they were to report immediately to the American government in Rastatt, Germany, where they would remain until their travel arrangements to America were finalized. The next day, they drove through Koblenz, Mainz, Worms, and Karlsruhe to reach the camp.

Saturday, John wrote to his mother, describing their new temporary home in Breman. Once again, he fabricated parts of the letter, adding good food and a fictional children's menu to make their situation sound more appealing.

"The camp is nice, within large and modern barracks. There is central heating everywhere, and hot and cold running water. The food is good, and they have a particularly good children's menu."

The next few months flew past in a blur of confusion and paperwork. John fully believed their trip plans would solidify, but they had postponed the dream so many times that he grew more agitated as the dates inched closer. Jarmila watched the light in his eyes and held her breath. She feared that, if their emigration fell through, John might never recover from the disappointment.

But this time, the halting cogs of bureaucracy churned forward. As the details of the trip came together, the Honolka family stood on the brink of the biggest adventure of their lives.

Ready to board the USS General Harry Taylor at Port Bremerhaven, Germany. From left to right: Lada, Eva holding Tommy's hand, John, Berta Marie "Omie" (John's mother who came to say goodbye), John Junior, Jarmila, and Vlasta The voyagers have tickets pinned to their coats with their travel numbers, instead of names.

Leaving from Bremerhaven, Germany on the USS General Harry Taylor, the Honolka family gathered on deck and watched from two arched windows. Most of the family is together in the center archway; Vlasta moved to the left archway where she could have a better view.

CHAPTER SEVENTEEN

THE VOYAGE BEGINS

They huddled together at the Bremerhaven, Germany, port, waiting to board the USS General Harry Taylor. The temperature was a chilly 50 degrees, with a cool breeze blowing off the North Sea. Jarmila filled her lungs with the fresh air. Nearly 3,500 refugees stared at the huge —522-foot-long ship. John did the calculations in his head—nearly 1.5 times the length of the Sparta football field.

Jarmila carried one-year-old Thomas. John held tightly to John Jr.'s hand to keep the four-year-old from running ahead.

Eva and Vlasta followed Lada, dragging the small suitcase that held the family's belongings. John's mother, Berta Marie, who the children referred to as "Omie," came to Bremerhaven to tell them goodbye.

"We'll be home again when it's safe. Maybe in four years. Like the blink of an eye. As soon as the political climate improves." John spoke optimistically, not knowing it would be forty years before his homeland would be free again, and the family would never return.

Hundreds of refugees filed onto the USS Taylor that morning—all fled their war-ravaged countries in search of a free life. They had risked everything, given up everything, to get to this point. Like the Honolkas, many spent years in prison or refugee camps. This moment was one they had dreamed of, fought for, and sacrificed for. Most had walked the last leg of this journey. They were bone-weary, with blistered feet. All tried to stand straight, tall and proud, with dignity. As they stood at that dock, the crowd murmured with anticipation. Something stirred within them. Jarmila's step was lighter. Her body, stronger. She searched for a word to define the feeling. At long last, she recognized the moment for what it represented—the revival of hope, but also the sense of grief at the loss of her home, her parents and siblings.

Not long after the ship reached open waters of the sea, they encountered a ferocious storm that rocked the vessel from side to side for hours. Jarmila and Eva became nauseated, as did many others. Rain poured from the skies to toss the ship mercilessly across the waves. So many people were ill that the sailors scattered sawdust on all the hallways for easier cleanup where the suffering travelers had vomited.

For most of the journey, the family endured sweltering heat. The quarters below deck were cramped and crowded, with no windows or fans to circulate the air. At night, only men and boys were allowed on the deck, where temperatures were slightly cooler. John did what he could to make the trip more bearable for his family—including disguising Vlasta as a boy and smuggling her onto the top deck to sleep each night.

The vessel's course took them from the English Channel to the South American city of Puerto de Cabello, Brazil. There, they docked briefly to restock supplies. People from the town swarmed to see the ship with the refugees and throw bananas to those on board. John tried, without success, to catch some for the children. Vlasta loved bananas, and it had been a long time since they had eaten fresh fruit.

After a two-week voyage on the open seas, they arrived at the Demarcation port of New Orleans on April 26, 1951. Their trip was one of more than 30 humanitarian transatlantic voyages the USS Harry Taylor would complete in the years following the war.

Jarmila's legs wobbled beneath her as she walked onto the gangplank carrying Thomas. Behind her, Lada dragged their one small suitcase. Eva and Vlasta followed next. John held John Jr. by the hand. Workers would unload their medium-sized faded red wooden crate later and take it to the train station. All wore broad grins when their feet hit the pavement at the Port of New Orleans.

"This is America," John said, "but it isn't where we will stay. Our land of opportunity is north of here, in Iowa. We will go there by train."

Officials directed the family to cattle-like pens, set up separating the refugees into designated waiting areas based on their destinations. Two women arrived with a car and drove them to the train station. They arrived mid-afternoon, along with swarms of other refugees.

With hope in their hearts, John and Jarmila followed the crowd into the New Orleans Train Station. They accepted a loaf of bread from American Red Cross volunteers and John tore chunks for each of them.

Together, they boarded a 1:45 p.m. train for the trip to Creston, Iowa, which would take them another 36 hours with dozens of stops along the way. Exhausted from the long voyage, the children slept in their seats for most of the journey. Periodic whistle blows interrupted the rhythm of the train, but the weary family barely heard them. Even the baby, Tom, woke only when he was hungry.

Jarmila and John took turns dozing to keep an eye on their children and their belongings. They ate meals provided by the volunteers from New Orleans or purchased with the small allotment of cash they had been given. John and Jarmila carefully rationed the food to make it last the distance. By the time the train rattled through Cedar Falls, Iowa, more than two days later, the food bag was empty, and their cash was gone.

Along the way, the number of refugees dwindled as they exited the train at earlier stops. Finally, the train pulled into Creston. It was late morning. Except for one thin man in his 70's, the depot was deserted. He wore a plaid shirt and faded denim overalls. A straw hat shaded his eyes as he watched John and Jarmila gather the children and their belongings. In his hands, the old man held a hand-written sign: Honolka.

Their American sponsors, a farmer and his wife, spoke Czech and English. John strode toward the man and shook his hand. The family followed him to a 1939 four-door Chevy, dark green and covered in dust from the gravel roads of the farmland. They loaded their suitcase and crate into the trunk and piled into the car.

Plowed fields stretched into the horizon on both sides of the road for as far as they could see. John and Jarmila stared at the vast farmland around them. They had been city people. Their new home was miles from any town. They bounced along the country roads, only occasionally seeing a farmhouse and barn.

"You can live on the property and work the fields," the farmer said.

John nodded. "That's what we agreed."

"Your salary is ten cents per hour."

John was silent.

An hour later, they arrived at the farmer's home, in Protivin, where they were to stay until they recovered from the long trip. They remained there for one week, resting in clean beds and eating good food. Then it was time to move into their own place. When Lada saw the dilapidated building, he burst out laughing. He nudged Vlasta. "Well, it has large windows, just like Mom wanted," he said.

Jarmila stood, speechless. She had dreamed of a cozy house with a modern kitchen and big windows. Most of the pictures she had seen of America portrayed a land of luxury, where people lived in new homes and drove nice cars. This was not what she expected. Not what any of them had expected.

John and Jarmila had prayed for a good life in a home where they could raise their children in peace and freedom. When their prayers were answered, they walked away from their families, and their homeland. They had already lost everything else to the Communists—their home, John's business, and some of their health, while living in the prisons and refugee camps. They came to America with little more than the clothes on their backs and a dream in their hearts.

Although some small part of her had hoped for more, Jarmila was prepared to begin their lives in a little house, perhaps with a yard where the kids could play. Instead, they found themselves dropped off at a weathered outbuilding on the edge of a cornfield. Jarmila stared at the building in disbelief.

The structure, built in the late 1800's, had been a shelter for the cows before they arrived. In front of the house, a windmill pumped water into a trough for the cattle to drink; an outdoor privy was close by.

At first glance, the surrounding yard was lovely, with many large shade trees, flowering trees, and fruit trees. A windbreak of trees lined one side of the property, next to a dilapidated old barn. However, the grass and weeds were knee-deep, and home to a wide variety of birds, snakes, and rodents. Cow chips were everywhere.

Jarmila walked inside their new home and covered her nose and mouth as she gagged from the stench of cow manure. The farmer had shooed the cows out of their shelter to prepare it for the Honolka family. The basement consisted of a dirt hole in the ground filled with rainwater. Cow chips covered the dirt floors. The building had no running water, toilet facilities, gas or electricity. There were large open spaces designated as windows, but only a few of them had glass.

The condition of the property was so foul that Jarmila could scarcely comprehend it. She had begun her life as an adored little girl who attended concerts and the theater. Her home had contained beautiful furnishings, original paintings, and nice carpets. In Czechoslovakia, she and John had lived in their own home. They were the first in their neighborhood to have a car. John built an opening into the basement for an underground garage, where the car could be parked next to the coal bins—unusual for the times.

Here, in this cow pasture, she had nothing. The furnishings were sparse. There was an old-fashioned wooden stove and a kerosene lantern. A rocking chair sat in one corner. A few necessary furnishings had been donated by farm families in Protivin—a table and chairs, pans, a broom, pillows and quilts. Jarmila studied her filthy surroundings, too stunned to comment. Something inside of her broke into a million pieces.

Finally, she opened the door of the icebox. There was no block of ice inside. She turned to her husband. "What are we supposed to do with this?"

John wrapped his arms around her. "We're here now. Let's make the best of it."

Together, the weary family raked the cow chips into a pile outside the house. They ate a light supper of the remaining provisions from the farmer and fell into bed before dark.

That night, as the children slept on the thin mattresses with blankets and pillows, a rare treat, Jarmila whispered to John.

"We are indentured servants in the land of golden opportunity. This is as bad as the camps we came from."

"We won't stay here, Jarmila. I will think of something."

The Honolka family first moved into this farm house, built in the late 1800's, which had been a shelter for the cows before they arrived. At the time, the windows had no glass and the floor was covered in manure.

CHAPTER EIGHTEEN

MAKING A HOME IN AMERICA

Summer of 1951

Early the next morning, the farmer came in his truck to take John and Lada to his home farm for work in the field and barn. Jarmila resolved to hide her disappointment from her children, but their new home looked no better than it had the first time they saw it. After John and Lada headed for the fields, she walked all the way around the house, surveying the peeling paint, faded and torn wallpaper, and sagging doors.

There was no drinking water. The cow trough water was to be used for cleaning, laundry, and bathing. The water for drinking and cooking was in an old tin milk can and had to be carried into town to be refilled with fresh, clean water.

Jarmila swallowed the lump in her throat before it could spill over into tears. Then, she and Eva went to work on the old farmhouse.

While John and Lada were away, Jarmila and Eva found a rake and a broom and cleared the floors of debris. Jarmila used a bar of bath soap and a handful of wet rags to wipe every surface. She cleared cobwebs from the corners. She scrubbed the old wooden table until her back throbbed and scoured the floor on her hands and knees.

With her house as clean as she could make it, Jarmila was determined to prepare a decent meal for her family. The farmer provided a hearty lunch for John and Lada, but Jarmila and the children had to fend for themselves.

John and Lada arrived from the fields at dusk, covered in dirt. They washed in the cow trough and rejoined the family.

John stood in the doorway and stared at the transformed farmhouse. The floors were clean and smooth. The table and countertops were spotless. The children wore fresh clothes and smiled up at him with shining faces. A pot of soup simmered on the wood stove. He shook his head at the miracle Jarmila had accomplished. "You have worked as hard in this house as we did in the fields."

As they shared their first home-cooked meal in America, Lada told of driving a tractor. He was not yet thirteen but had worked the full day for no pay—just a field hand lunch with good food, and lots of it. "We had something called 'pie' for dessert," he announced. "It was delicious. Filled with sweet fruit. Mine was an apple pie, but they said it can also be filled with cherries or almost anything. You need the recipe, Mother. You will love pie!"

That first day was the hardest. Word of the struggling immigrant family traveled fast in the small town. Most everyone knew of the landowner who sponsored them, and his frugal reputation. On Sunday after church, one of the area farmers invited the family to their home for dinner. Afterwards, they sent the leftovers with their guests—along with a welcome gift of groceries. One of those farmers introduced Vlasta to Jello mixed with fruit cocktail, a treat she still loves today.

John and Jarmila happily accepted the food they received from the townsfolk, which sometimes included fresh eggs, or a chicken Jarmila could bake into a delicious meal. But the kindness of strangers couldn't change the living conditions on the farm. Filth surrounded them. Every day, Jarmila cleaned. Every day, more dust blew through the open windows to fall in thick piles throughout the farmhouse. One day, John cleaned out the farmer's barn and arrived home with his hands, boots, and hair caked in manure. "The barn was so full of stinking waste that the cows couldn't walk through it," he said.

It wasn't long before the old milk tin ran out of water. Lada and Vlasta walked to town to refill it. A neighboring farmer stopped to give them a ride in his pickup truck to the town. After they filled it, the two children dragged the heavy container all the way home on their own. Sometimes a farmer driving by the two children would give them a ride to town and back, their old milk tin filled with fresh water. As word got out, farmers in the area brought fresh water, eggs, meat, and vegetables to welcome the newcomers.

Lada and Vlasta worked hard but also devised their own entertainment. Once they found a rope to hang from the rafters of the barn, where they had fun swinging from one side of the old building to the other.

At the end of the month, John wrote to tell his mother the family had arrived in America. Berta had believed in her son, supported their dreams of freedom, and funded much of their journey. John couldn't bear to disappoint her with the truth. Instead, he painted a rosy picture of their journey on the USS Harry Taylor.

"The food on the ship was particularly good," he wrote. "In the morning, they had coffee, scrambled eggs, bread, porridge and compote. Lunch: potatoes, meat (plenty), salad, and compote. For tea, one apple or orange. For dinner: potatoes, meat, vegetables, fruit, tea and bread—you could take as much as you wanted. There was a special menu for small children. There was no hunger."

Jarmila disapproved. "You shouldn't lie to your mother. The food was good, but not all was as you have written.

"If I tell her what really happened, she will despair that all her sacrifices were wasted."

"Then write about the true things that are good."

John raised one eyebrow. "We don't have enough of those to fill a letter."

"I can't wait to see how you describe our house," she said.

John bent over the page again. He wrote of the generosity of the American Red Cross and the food they provided. He told of driving through the city in a beautiful limousine to arrive at the train station.

"Traveling by train is also pleasant," he said. "There are only padded seats in the United States, with the seats facing the direction of travel. There is cooled drinking water and every comfort in every car."

Before he wrote about their new home, he paused to think. He imagined his mother sitting alone in the small apartment she and his father had shared after their forced removal from their Czechoslovakian home. He decided he would tell her the true story another time. For now, a few small lies might comfort her.

"Our guarantor has two cars and a truck. There is no farmer here without a car – the nicest, biggest cars. You do not see anyone walking by foot. Our farmer has three tractors. I drive the biggest one, which has nine speeds. Corn is now being planted. Since school is already on break here, Lada has learned to drive a small tractor. It is a lot of fun for him.

"The food here is first class everywhere. . .for lunch and dinner, we have meat, chickens, geese, compotes, pastries, and always coffee. We have it nice around our house now. We have a large garden—as big as the garden in Trutnov. We have some forest. We have a lot of wood to burn. The fruit trees are now blooming, and lots of roses. The children could not have it any better. Tomik can walk alone and will not need to be afraid that something will happen to him."

The truth was somewhat different. Yes, Lada learned to drive a tractor, but only because he had to do field work. There was no garden. The "forest" was the row of trees that provided a windbreak. The roses didn't exist, and John had neglected to mention the weeds that filled their yard. Thomas could not walk by himself—but John stretched the story so his mother would not worry. He read his own words and decided it might be wise to add more about the adjustments required to live in a new country.

"Jarmila is a bit scared, but she will get used to it, too. There are a lot of Czechs around us, even one of the church services is in Czech. Eva goes to school in Protivin, Iowa. She is being taught by a nun. Eva speaks German to her."

John ended his letter with the one thing he wanted his mother to believe:

"For the time being, you do not have to worry. We live unbelievably beautiful and healthy lives."

The stories John wrote to his mother contradicted the conditions he described in his communication with the immigration authorities. He wrote those officials a letter requesting his family's return to their homeland. He noted their living arrangements, the work hours, and pay. He implored them to act quickly, because the family couldn't survive the Iowa winter in the house they had been provided.

People in the community were still talking about the record 19.9 inches of snow that had fallen on Cedar Rapids in March—just two months before John and his family moved to Iowa. Without heat, the Honolka family would freeze to death when the wind and snow blew through the open windows. The Washington, D.C., Council for Czechoslovakia had never received such a request before—generally people who had suffered the hardships of war were happy to arrive in the land of freedom.

The council investigated. Soon, they arranged for a different sponsor—the Milo Naxera family, who owned a bakery in Cedar Rapids, Iowa. By fall, their debt to the old farmer was settled. They moved to a house in Walford, eighteen miles southwest of Cedar Rapids and 115 miles south of the dismal farmhouse they had first inhabited. It was a temporary home, owned by a relative of the Naxera's, but it would provide shelter until a more permanent home became available. The house was a nice one, with electricity and running water, but no indoor toilet. A privy was nearby. The yard was clean, with a grassy lawn. Without a car, John relied on his neighbors to drive him into Cedar Rapids each day, where he worked at Andrew Polehna's meat market. Jarmila and the children were alone in the small town while John worked to feed them.

The three oldest children—Eva (15), Lada (13), Vlasta (10)—started school in Walford, where they began learning to improve their English. Eva was humiliated to be placed in a fourth-grade class, where her teachers felt she would have a better opportunity to learn the language and the way of life in America. In Walford, Vlasta made her first American friend, Patty Bessey, who taught her to speak English, beginning with "flower" as her first word.

The little girl also introduced Vlasta to others, including her in Halloween activities with schoolmates.

Johnny (5), stayed home with Jarmila and baby Thomas. On Saturdays, Eva rode to Cedar Rapids with John. She worked at the Naxera bakery, doing janitorial work and cleaning the apartment above the bakery, the Naxera's residence. The job paid $5 and one sack of leftover pastries.

Jarmila cooked a hot breakfast every morning, sent the children off to school, and had the house sparkling when John came home at night. On the surface, their lives had improved. Only John and their daughter Eva noticed a change in Jarmila.

Eva spoke to her father about it one Saturday after she finished her shift at the bakery and he was home from the meat market.

"Matka (Mother) is sad. She is quiet all the time. She pretends to smile, but it never reaches her eyes."

Her father didn't argue. "She is homesick for Czechoslovakia."

"It's more than that," Eva said. "She's alone all the time. She doesn't even play her music anymore."

Eva's observations were good ones. There was nothing but work to occupy her mother. She would have enjoyed playing a violin but didn't have one. She had no radio and no friends to talk to. Occasionally, Jarmila entertained herself with a harmonica she bought for herself in a music store.

"Maybe she is tired of the struggles," John told his daughter. "Things will be better soon."

"I hope so," Eva replied.

CHAPTER NINETEEN

HAMILTON STREET

Within a few months, the Honolkas relocated again—this time, to Cedar Rapids. They settled at 1507 Hamilton Street, in the Czech area of Cedar Rapids on 16th Avenue. The house belonged to relatives of the Andrew Polehna family, Czechs willing to help fellow immigrants from their homeland. On 16th Avenue, a block away from their new home, Czech-speaking businesses lined the street; there, the older generation primarily spoke Czech.

At last, nearly five months after they had arrived in America, the Honolkas lived in a cozy house with a potbelly coal stove in the center of the home, the dining room where everyone gathered. The Polehna and Naxera families, and a few other Czech people, donated furniture for the house.

The two sisters shared one bedroom; Lada and John Jr. were in another. John and Jarmila kept young Thomas in their bedroom, where he shared their bed until they could find him a crib. In the evenings, Eva turned on her radio, and the girls listened to soap operas in their bedroom, one of many new experiences.

This was the home Jarmila had longed for in America. Here, they felt like a real family again. Eva, Lada, Vlasta and little John Jr. enrolled at St. Wenceslaus School Parish, where many Czech descendants' children attended. The kindergarten class was located on the first floor of the two-story brick building, which was fortunate for Johnny. On his first day of school, he promptly jumped out of the window and ran home.

John sought out people who spoke Czech, German, Polish or French, to network with others who had immigrated to the region, or who had ties to his homeland. Someone suggested he visit the nearby Amana Colonies for German-speaking residents, and John drove there to see the shops. He struck up a conversation in German with the manager of the general store in Main Amana, Fred Geiger. It was another of John's connections who would become a close friend over time.

Still, life was difficult. John and Jarmila instilled high work ethics in all their children. One evening, when the three older children had been in school for less than a week, John gazed around the dinner table, eyes resting briefly on each one before nodding to Jarmila.

She cleared her throat and claimed their attention. "Listen to your father. This is important."

All eyes turned to John, who addressed the family in a serious tone. "Here in America, we have opportunities and responsibilities," he said. "We must all do our best at both. This means that you children will go to school, where you have the opportunity to learn. But you will also work, because you have a responsibility to contribute to your family."

"Who will hire me?" Ten-year-old Vlasta's serious little face stared back at her father.

"Not all work pays money," John said. "Your job will be to help your mother. When she does the laundry, you can fold clothes. When she cleans the house, you can help. We will find ways for you to do both school and work."

Everyone in the Honolka family worked.

At 15, Eva had two jobs. After school each afternoon, she walked to a house across the street from St. Wenceslaus School, where she babysat three children until their parents arrived home from work. When she finished, she walked an hour to Noxera's bakery, to clean the bakery after it closed. Then she walked another hour and a half home. Her payment was an hourly wage and an occasional bag of baked goods.

Lada, who had changed his name to "Don" to be more American, worked after school for Polehna's Meat Market. John brought large sacks of garlic home for Don to peel and returned the cloves to the butcher shop to be used for the sausages and salami. In this way, Don earned the money for his first bicycle.

Vlasta learned to mow grass, weed gardens, trim and water plants and yards. One summer, while other people were on vacation, she also went corn de-tasseling—all to earn money for her school clothes and shoes.

Winter arrived with a blast of snow that blanketed the city and carried through to the holidays. That December, Eva sang in the St. Wenceslaus church choir. A Cedar Rapids radio station interviewed her for a Christmas program broadcast in Czech. The family gathered around their RCA radio to listen.

Money was tight that winter. Although John worked long hours—and Jarmila and Eva contributed with their earnings—the family sent a small portion of every dollar back home to both parents. After John and Jarmila escaped from the Communists, their families were targeted for retribution. Jarmila's parents had been respected middle-class business owners. Her father owned a cobbler shop and the couple lived in a nice home, with a courtyard and a few geese. They made a decent living until the Communists confiscated their business and their home, moved them into a tiny one-bedroom apartment, and issued them a small monthly stipend—barely enough to keep them alive.

Each month, Jarmila received a new letter from home, heavily redacted by Communist censors. Sometimes the letter would have half of it inked out, so it was not readable. Black marks struck through large portions of the message, but the censors never deleted requests for medicine and financial support. John suspected the government agents knew the immigrants would send money to those they had left behind. They were right. And, when those letters arrived with money inside, the censors confiscated the cash before delivering the letters.

Still, John and Jarmila couldn't bear to think of Jarmila's parents going without their medications after all they had done to support their relocation to America. As a final affront, the Communists forced Jarmila's father to work in a factory until he became ill and could no longer work. Fighting esophageal cancer with no reprieve from the government, he still refused to join the Communist Party. The money John and Jarmila sent for medicine never arrived. Both of Jarmila's parents died penniless and alone under the cruel regime.

Two nights before Christmas, after the children were asleep, Jarmila sat in her chair, knitting a Christmas scarf for Vlasta. John bent over the kitchen table, writing a letter to his mother. The potbelly stove warmed the living area between them. Jarmila heard footsteps on the porch. Someone knocked quietly on their door. John went to answer it. Several friends from St. Wenceslaus Church stood waiting. A sturdy woman wearing a red woolen coat spoke first.

"We're here to deliver your Christmas," she said. "May we come inside?"

John opened the door wide, and the jolly bunch carried in a Christmas tree, which they decorated with 24 electric candles and a box of ornaments. Beneath the tree, they arranged boxes of gifts from the Sisters at St. Wenceslaus School. There were new rain boots for each child, plus a basket filled with preserves, chocolate, bananas and other foods.

On December 26th, John wrote to his mother about their first American Christmas. He described the huge snowfall that had blanketed Cedar Rapids, setting the mood for the holiday. *We had a nice Christmas,* he wrote. *We got gifts from our friends, and I cannot list everything. Eva has received a new radio, Honzik (Johnny) and Thomas mechanical toys, a Christmas tree with electric lights because they do not have candles here. We did not need anything this time because we got everything.*

Jarmila also wrote home after Christmas. Her letter overflowed with gratitude to the many American friends who surprised the family with their generosity. *I did not look forward to Christmas at all,* she wrote. *I had quite large expenses due to our emigration. Therefore, we had little money left for Christmas. But everything turned out differently.*

She described the gifts from the St. Wenceslaus school, from the Naxera family who owned the local bakery, and from friends in New Orleans and Durham. She told of the abundance of thoughtful presents—from shoes and socks to roller skates, silk scarfs and perfume to fountain pens and toys. The Honolkas had received candy dishes and a coffee maker, cowboy hats, and wallets. There were ice skates for Lada and Vlasta, and a new gray suit for John. Thomas received a wooden workbench with hammers and screws, along with a talking teddy bear, a tractor, and a toy tank. Eva treasured her new brush, mirror, and comb set. Two Czech refugee men stopped by with an electric shaver for John and more gifts for the children.

"We are incredibly grateful for these good people," Jarmila wrote. *"We did not expect that. People in America are very generous. America is an extraordinarily rich country."*

Eva studied her mother's face each day, searching for the joyful woman she once knew. Slowly, Eva watched Jarmila's spirits improve. Jarmila sewed curtains for the little house. She worked hard and often made home-baked goods for the nuns at St. Wenceslaus in appreciation for the help they gave her children. The nuns loved her baked goods, especially the jelly-filled Bismarck's. One evening, Eva came home to see her mother playing the harmonica for little Thomas. She sat down to listen.

When Jarmila finished, the children applauded.

"Music makes me happy," Eva said.

"I've always enjoyed it."

"What is your favorite instrument, mom?"

Jarmila cocked her head to ponder the question before she answered. "Probably the violin, because I have played it for the longest time. But each instrument is different. I like all of them: the harmonica, the accordion, all instruments."

The meat market found a good employee in John Honolka. He arrived early, worked late, and befriended his coworkers and customers. Everyone loved John. When he arrived home at night, he often brought home a string of "parkie" wieners, nicknamed from the Czech word "parek." The kids considered them a treat.

Lada stuffed a large bite of a parek into his mouth. "I could eat these every night," he said.

"Me, too." Five-year-old John Jr. admired anything his big brother said or did.

"Boys, don't talk with your mouth full," Jarmila scolded.

But John marveled at the difference a full belly made in his children. "It's a good problem to have, eh, Jarmila?"

With John's access to the meat market's unsold inventory at reduced prices, the family nearly always had meat for dinner. Jarmila cooked some of their favorites from their beloved Czechoslovakia—wiener schnitzel, and goulash. On cold evenings, they gathered around the potbelly stove to keep warm.

"Let me feed it," John Jr. begged.

Lada helped the little boy shovel a scoop of coal into the fire.

But John couldn't spend the evening at home with his family because he had a night janitorial job in a factory. A new Square-D had been built in Cedar Rapids and John's job was to clean the windows and anything else that needed cleaning. Square-D was in the opposite direction of Polehna's Meat Market, so John walked the long distance from one job to the other.

He was an educated, successful businessman in his homeland. Here, he became a butcher and a janitor. What would be next? He willingly gave it all for freedom.

CHAPTER TWENTY

GROWING UP IN AMERICA

Somehow, in between their jobs and raising their family, John and Jarmila found ways to spend individual time with each of their children. One Saturday after work, John scooped up John Jr. and Thomas and took them on a bus trip to downtown Cedar Rapids. The movie "Fort Apache" was playing at the Paramount Theater. Johnny and Thomas stared up at John Wayne on the big screen and fell in love with cowboys and Indians. The show ended after dark. John hustled the boys onto the last bus ride of the night. Both fell sound asleep on the ride home.

With the passing of each day, the Honolka children grew more confident in their new surroundings. They learned the language, made new friends, and devoured the food. Although Jarmila felt they were growing up too fast, she was proud of their resilience. On the rare nights when John and Jarmila had a few minutes to themselves, they assessed their progress.

"Zatím to ujde," John said. So far, so good.

"Mladí se snadno přizpůsobí." The young adapt easily.

For Jarmila, the transition was more difficult. Aware of the heavy toll their Czechoslovakian relatives still paid in their homeland, she could not allow herself to enjoy the abundance spread before them. With every free breath she took, Jarmila felt the weight of guilt on her chest. While she and John enjoyed a new life of freedom in America, her parents had been forced to give up their own lives and her father's business as a cobbler. Her brother was imprisoned, sentenced to a life of hard labor. Jarmila longed for her family, her language, her customs, her beloved mountains and forests, and her home.

The America that welcomed John and Jarmila in the 50s was a happy one. Memories of The Great Depression were fading. The post-war economy was soaring. Soldiers were home. Families built homes in the suburbs and gathered their children around them to watch programs like Hopalong Cassidy and Topper on their black-and-white television sets.

John bought a used tabletop RCA-TV and brought it home to Thomas, so he would have some fun, too. Tom was small, frail, and sickly. He spent his time at home with his mother while the three older children had after-school jobs or commitments. John hoped Honzik (John Jr.) and Tommy would enjoy the TV together. "It is the cheapest way to learn English," John said, "and you never have to leave your home."

John and Jarmila watched a few TV programs together in the evenings, when possible. Occasionally, they went downtown to the Cedar Rapids coliseum to watch professional wrestling. One night, Jarmila became too excited when her favorite wrestler was being abused. She took off her shoe and threw it at the abuser. The shoe landed in the center of the ring. The match had to be stopped while everyone waited for the guilty person to come forward and claim their shoe. Jarmila's escapade made her a star on the evening news the following day.

Dwight D. Eisenhower ran for US President in 1952, rolling into victory on his reputation as a five-star general and Supreme Allied Commander during WWII. "Ike" had acted as a Chief of Staff for the Army under President Harry Truman, the governor of U.S. occupied Germany after WWII, the president of Columbia University and the Supreme Commander of NATO forces. Throughout Cedar Rapids, everyone wore "I LIKE IKE" campaign buttons. It came as no surprise when Republican Eisenhower and his running mate Richard Nixon defeated the "intellectual candidate" Democrat Adlai Stevenson with a total of 442 electoral votes to 89 and a popular vote of 54.9 percent to 44.4 percent.[xxvi]

Cedar Rapids had a thriving Czech community in the 50s, centered around 16th Avenue SW and 3rd Street SE. People referred to the neighborhood as the Bohemia Town. So many Czechs lived, worked and shopped in this area that many store owners displayed signs printed in both English and Czech. Store clerks often spoke Czech; even the sidewalk crossing lights gave instructions in both languages.

The Honolka family attended Czechoslovakian church services at St. Wenceslaus Church, one of the city's oldest and most beautiful. Eva and Vlasta sang in the choir while colored beams from the stained-glass windows cast a glow across the altar and pews. During the weekdays, the children attended the St. Wenceslaus school and sometimes went to church before going to class.

Although they lived in an area surrounded by their Czech heritage and people, Jarmila kept to herself. She had always been reserved around others; now she struggled with a lack of self-confidence. Jarmila felt her English wasn't fluent enough. She rarely left their home other than to go to work; John did some of the shopping after he finished his regular work schedule. Eva saw her mother's hesitation and did her best to help. Jarmila rarely had time to socialize, but she joined an artistic group of Czechs, who performed Czech plays on stage, traveling by car to different Iowa towns to perform. This provided Jarmila with a little social life.

In January of 1953, Dwight D. Eisenhower was inaugurated as the 34th President of the United States of America. The winter was frigid in Cedar Rapids. Temperatures hovered around 26 degrees during the warmest part of the day, with winds at 14 miles-per-hour. During the winter, it was Don's job to get up early in the morning and take the coal bucket to the garage to fill it with coal for the potbelly stove. John always started the fire and made the house warm for the rest of the family when they got up in the morning; before he left for work, on foot.

No matter how much they bundled up, the Honolka children froze on their walk to school and back each day. The family gathered around the potbelly stove every night, seeking a repricve from the snowy Iowa weather. Nights were long during those winter months. Eva was sixteen. As Jarmila retreated to the shelter of her home, Eva stepped into the spotlight. Lada was two years behind her in school, and Vlasta was two behind her brother. Teachers at St. Wenceslaus counted on Eva to deliver messages or paperwork to her parents—whether it pertained to her own education, or one of her siblings.

At fourteen, Don often stayed after school for athletics. He had transferred to Wilson High School the previous year because St. Wenceslaus had no sports programs. Don naturally excelled in all sports, and his determination and work ethic won the respect of his coaches. He didn't play football, but he ran track and played basketball. With Jarmila's encouragement, he and Eva both joined SOKOL gymnastics and spent many cold, snowy evenings at practice. The SOKOL program traced its roots to 1862 Czechoslovakia. Jarmila had participated in SOKOL as a young girl, and was pleased to see her children involved in the same activities she had enjoyed. The word "sokol" translates to falcon and is symbolic of the SOKOL ideals: Courage, Strength, Endurance, Fraternalism, Love of democratic principles, and Pride in country.

Don consistently won in his athletic competitions during 1954 and 1955, advancing to district championships representing 6-8 states. One year, he competed in ten sports against 2,000 athletes, winning the gold medal overall. He stood proudly on the podium in the Cedar Rapids SOKOL Hall to receive his medal. When he presented it to his mother, Jarmila cried.

In addition to gymnastics, Eva joined her mother to perform in the Czech plays on stage. Vlasta spent her free time in the winter ice skating at Riverside Park, just three blocks from their home. The ice rink was lighted at night and had a small warm-up shack with a potbelly stove similar to the one in the Honolka dining room.

As their circumstances improved, John and Jarmila found ways to introduce Honzik and Thomas to American customs and history. John bought a 1950 dark green, four-door Plymouth big enough for the whole family to take short road trips to see nearby attractions and towns. One Sunday, John took the family on an excursion an hour east of Cedar Rapids, to a small town called Tama. The children's chatter faded away as they watched rolling crops fly past their window. Johnny and Thomas heard the drumbeats before they pulled into a dusty parking lot on the outskirts of the town.

"Indians!" they shouted.

John and Jarmila smiled at the boys' excitement.

"It's called a Pow Wow," John said. "This is where the Indians celebrate their heritage. Every dance has a meaning. Every song is passed down from their ancestors."

"These people are the real Native Americans," Eva said.

"Naked Americans!" Tommy giggled.

"Not naked, Tommy. Native," Eva said. "They were the first people to be here, before it was named America. This is their homeland."

Both boys were excited at the prospect of seeing live Indians. The family piled out of the car and walked through the Indian village with all the teepees and watched the squaws make Indian bread. Then they moved toward the crowded bleachers. For the next two hours, they watched the costumed performers in their rhythmic chanting, shuffling dance. Lada admired the horses and Jarmila studied the women. All wore massive bracelets and brass jewelry around their necks and ears. She admired the many colors and the feathers that adorned their hair.

In the center of the arena, a large man with long gray braids and a towering headdress pounded on a 24-inch drum. Intricate turquoise beadwork decorated the band, and long strands of leather fringe hung from his vest. The pageantry included costumed men, women and children, all dressed in bright colors and covered in paint and feathers. Even the horses wore headdresses and colorful blankets. During one dramatic ensemble, the entire tribe danced in magnificent rhythm. They sang in their native tongue as they snaked in single file into a circle around the drummer.

John answered the children's questions. "There are no arrows or hatchets. But there might be a bonfire later. These Pow Wows can go on for days.

Unfortunately, we must be home again in time for supper." They drove home in the dark.

The excursion was one that Johnny and Thomas never forgot. For the next several days, they whooped and hollered as they played cowboys and Indians with a renewed vigor, streaking their faces with mud, and poking stray chicken feathers into their hair. Theirs was a typical idyllic family life for Americans in the 50s. With every passing day, the children grew more "American" and their mother grew increasingly worried about the parents she had left behind.

CHAPTER TWENTY-ONE

POST WAR OPTIMISM

1953-55

With Stalin still in power in Russia, John Honolka realized his goal of returning to Czechoslovakia was not likely to happen as quickly as he had hoped. Each month, more US servicemen returned home from World War II in search of safety and security. Marriage and family life were at the top of everyone's mind. The economy was booming. Jobs were plentiful. Building a close-knit family was the fastest way to put the uncertainties of war into the past, where they belonged.

The number of marriages in America rose at an unprecedented rate, followed quickly by a housing boom. The 1950s brought the construction of around 13 million new homes, to house the young families. By the end of the 1950s, no less than 15 million units were under construction nationwide. Although a few women held jobs, society clearly expected men to be the family breadwinner—anyone who watched television or read Good Housekeeping magazine could verify that.[xxvii]

Life fell into a routine for John and Jarmila. They worked hard, raised their children, and sent small amounts of money home to their family in Czechoslovakia. It seemed there was never enough to go around. The frigid winter cast a bleak spell on the family. In Iowa, and all across America, society embraced the traditional family: working husband, stay-at-home mother, and well-behaved children. On television, The Adventures of Ozzie and Harriett captured the hearts and minds of viewers. The nation, eager to put the dark days of WWII into the past, embraced a lighter, rosier way of life. A new spirit of optimism and hope filled the air. Congress worked to portray U.S.

capitalism as morally superior to Soviet Communism. On June 14, 1954, President Eisenhower signed a bill to insert the phrase "under God" into the U.S. Pledge of Allegiance. It was a move the Honolka family wholeheartedly supported.

Jarmila, who had once discarded her dream of millinery design, still loved to study fashions. With dozens of new fabrics available after the war, she was eager to try them. She shopped at stores in the "Bohemi Town" and in downtown Cedar Rapids and smoothed her fingers over the soft taffeta, nylon, and rayon fabrics, but could not afford them. Jarmila often commented on how beautiful the fabrics were, and that she wished they were available when she was young. She was only in her thirties, but she already felt old, due to the harsh experiences of the last five years and before. John bought her a new portable Pfaff sewing machine, and she used it to modernize some of the donated clothing given to the children.

Though Jarmila fit perfectly into the role of stay-at-home mother, she understood the economics that drove other women into the workforce. She treasured her time with her children, loved to cook, and enjoyed cleaning her house. While some wives were chafing at their restrictive roles as homemakers, Jarmila counted her blessings. She was grateful to have a home to clean.

On top of her responsibilities as wife and mother, Jarmila found ways to contribute to the family's income. She took in weekly batches of ironing for women who found her through word-of-mouth. Every evening after the local radio station, KPLS, closed, Jarmila cleaned their downtown office. She spent hours dusting, polishing desks, mopping floors, and sanitizing toilets. Vlasta often tagged along to help. The radio station was a 45-minute walk in the city. The two set out after dinner and finished the job to return home in the dark most nights.

One night in 1954, after they cleaned the radio station and locked the door, the two walked across the 3rd Avenue Bridge to the Paramount Movie Theater to see *Gone with the Wind,* newly released in the widescreen format.

Jarmila had talked about the book many times and now the movie was playing. They attended the last showing of the day. Leaving the theater at midnight, they walked home again, arriving at 1 a.m. Both loved the movie and chatted about it all the way home, where Jarmila closed the door quietly behind them and they tiptoed past the living room to their bedrooms.

During his two-term presidency, Eisenhower created the U.S. highway system, strengthened Social Security, eased tensions with the U.S.S.R., created NASA, helped to fully de-segregate the Armed Forces, and signed some of the first modern civil rights laws. On May 17, 1954, in a landmark decision in the case of Brown v. Board of Education of Topeka, Kansas, the U.S. Supreme Court declared state laws establishing separate public schools for students of different races to be unconstitutional.[xxviii] John and Jarmila watched President Eisenhower's actions with cautious approval. They knew first-hand, how quickly the political climate could change.

The fall of 1954, Elvis Presley's hit song "That's All Right," played on the radio and girls at St. Wenceslaus High School raced to the record store to buy it. The nuns preferred their students listened to Doris Day and Perry Como, but once Elvis rock-n-rolled onto the music charts, there was no turning back. It wasn't long before Elvis Presley and Marilyn Monroe became youth icons, with more youngsters wanting to be like them. The boys gravitated to jeans and leather jackets, while the girls wore trendy pedal pushers and black and white saddle shoes.

Elvis did not impress Jarmila. She blushed when she talked about him; she felt his shaking and wiggling were indecent. During those early years, Jarmila preferred the children avoid the influence of rock and roll. Eva listened, but Vlasta did not. In time, even Jarmila decided she liked Elvis, too.

Eva loved music and followed Doris Day and Perry Como. She had a boyfriend and went to movies frequently. She liked Hollywood fashions and movie stars. In the three years since she'd arrived at St. Wenceslaus, Eva had become fluent in English, but she rarely spoke of the atrocities she'd known in her childhood. To most of her high school friends, Eva was pretty and fun-loving. She simply looked at life differently than they did, through the filter of her experiences. As a result, she spoke with a wisdom that occasionally made her teenage friends uncomfortable, but it was a Christian atmosphere, and they accepted her as she was.

Eva lived each day in gratitude for the freedoms her adopted country provided. She had little patience for those who took those freedoms for granted. If Eva had expressed her opinions unkindly, her audience might have rejected them as spiteful criticism. Instead, she inspired people of all age. Eva gained the admiration of her teachers and the loyalty of her classmates.

In January 1955, the Cedar Rapids Gazette asked Eva to share her experiences in an interview. The result was an article that established the young girl as a spokesperson for freedom. Russ Wiley, the staff writer, captured Eva's story:

Eva Honolka, 17, is free to select a book of her choice from the library at St. Wenceslaus High School. That freedom is part of the reward she and her family won by escaping from Communist-controlled Czechoslovakia.

Trouble-tossed teenage years as a Czech displaced person might well have taught only lessons of bitterness and hatred to 17-year-old Eva Honolka.

But Eva, safe today in Cedar Rapids, Iowa, would rather talk about youthful responsibilities in character building and about the unexplored areas of man's love for fellow man.

Eva may seem a little critical of some of the things she sees going on around her in America. But that criticism is understood when you know all of Eva's story.

Having a party dress is nice. But Eva has known the years when just a spark of hope seemed awfully big.

"Girls here say clothes make the girl. If you buy beautiful clothes, you will be beautiful. That is wrong. The first thing is to build good character. Then you will be pretty."

"Another thing," added Eva. "Lots of money and fun. That's all you hear. So many American boys and girls spend all their money on clothes and fun. Why don't they take a dollar or two every week and give it to people that need it more than they do?"

Eva likes her classes at St. Wenceslaus. She lives with her family in a southwest side home. She loves music, dancing, and art—although artwork is the only one she is financially able to practice.

Eva told of the family's home in Czechoslovakia, her father's business, and their lives before World War II.

"My mother was planning to send me to ballet school and buy a piano. I was 12 years old. But suddenly we had lost everything, and we were trying to escape."

She described the Communist takeover and her father's refusal to accept their way of life. She expressed her pride in her father's decision, the pain her family suffered when they were imprisoned, and the fear they experienced while they were separated from each other. In vivid detail, Eva told of their years in displaced persons camps, their efforts to emigrate, and their long journey to America.

In the final paragraphs of the article, Eva looked toward the future.

"In two years," said Eva, "I'll get my citizenship. That will be another big event in my life. I'm willing to work hard and want to do well here." She said she believed it's twice as easy to do well in America, compared to Europe. *"Here,"* she said, *"All you have to do is show ability and interest, and someone will help you. A teacher sees that a student has talent and arranges a scholarship for him. There is nothing like that in Europe."*

Eva concluded with a message of gratitude.

"All of us will never be able to repay or thank all the people that have helped us," she said.

When the people of Cedar Rapids read the teenager's story, they, too, were inspired. Several organizations invited Eva to speak. She willingly agreed. Her future career as a motivational speaker had already begun.

That winter was another cold one. The family spent many frigid nights huddled around the potbelly stove to stay warm. They shared news about work and school and watched Gunsmoke on the little black and white television set. Even John liked Gunsmoke.

By now, John, a college graduate and former business owner, worked as a produce clerk in the Daniel's Park Grocery Store, a butcher at the meat market, and a janitor for two different businesses. He performed all four jobs every day, six days a week, from 5 a.m. until 10 p.m. Jarmila did the same—between her ironing jobs, her janitorial work, and raising their children, she worked as many hours as her husband. If the children needed an example of hard work, they had only to look at their parents.

When Don asked if John still believed there was gold in the streets of America, John answered, "Yes." He taught his children, "There is gold if you are not too lazy to bend over and pick it up. It lies in the promise that America offers for you to work as a free man and pursue happiness with hope."

John was everything in America that he had been in Czechoslovakia: honest, trustworthy, tenacious, disciplined, and dedicated. He shared his work philosophy with his children daily. "An aggressive man will work today and play tomorrow," he told them. "But a lazy man will play today and work tomorrow. Always remember that a 12-hour day is only a half day's work."

Although he stressed the importance of work, John also encouraged his children to pursue other interests, in athletics or the outdoors. One day, John pulled two tickets out of his pocket.

"How would you like to go see a real football game, Tommy?"

"Just you and me?"

"Yep. We'll take the train from Marion to Chicago, all the way to Soldier Field."

"Yes!"

They sat together in the bleachers and watched the German football club from Stuttgart play the Chicago All Stars. It was a trip Tommy never forgot.

CHAPTER TWENTY-TWO

THE AMANA BAKERY

John's busy work schedule never prevented him from reading the *Cedar Rapids Gazette*. He always combed the newspaper to learn the national news, but also to find additional ways to earn money. One evening in June 1955, he studied the classified ads more closely. As he sat at the kitchen table with the newspaper in his hands, John's eye landed on a new advertisement.

"This is the one! This is the job for me." The ad read: Amana Bakery for Sale.

Although John had visited the General Store in Main Amana several times, he knew little about the Amana Colonies or the close-knit society that started the bakery generations earlier. He only knew he wanted an opportunity to prove himself. He had the knowledge and experience to grow the bakery, if only he could buy it.

He called the next morning to make an appointment to discuss the sale of the bakery. John longed to be independent again. He had worked four years in America, waiting for this moment. The receptionist described the bakery as a small business in Upper South Amana just 19 miles southwest of Cedar Rapids.

If John had researched the community, he might have discovered the society was a religious community that originated in Germany. About 1,200 members settled in Iowa, named their new community Amana, meaning "to remain true," and incorporated as a society that believed in communal property.

They opposed military service, taking oaths, amusement, and a paid ministry. Members gave up all their property to a common fund and, in return, the corporation promised them economic security for their lifetime. They began with six Amana villages in 1859. In 1861, they added a seventh village Homestead, giving the colony access to the railroad.

In those early years, the community shared all property and resources. The village council of elders, who ran both the spiritual and business affairs of the colony, assigned all adults a job. The community supported itself through farming and the production of wool and calico. They became well known for their high-quality craftsmanship of everything from clocks to beer, to woolen goods.

The Amana Colonies had limited contact with the outside world. For several decades, the communal way of life worked well. Then, people realized they had to modernize because productivity declined as the younger generations grew. After the Great Depression of 1929, they reorganized to separate their religious and economic interests. The Amana Society, Inc., became a profit-sharing corporation to manage the farmland, mills, and other enterprises. The Amana Church Society continued pietistic traditions, emphasizing Bible study and prayer. They conducted worship services in German. The society shrank to 500 members in four churches.

When John arrived for his interview, the Amana Colonies were twenty years into the newly restructured system. Although they had voted for the changes in order to survive, many were still adjusting to their new way of life. Members still held conservative religious beliefs, which made it difficult for them to accept the idea of free enterprise and personal gain. Unaware of the Amana Society's long history of communal life—which discouraged private ownership of any business—John made the short drive to the address listed in the ad. The bakery was on top of a hill in a large, two-story red brick building in Upper South Amana (up the hill from South Amana).[xxix] At the time, Upper South Amana included one barn, three old brick homes, one new modern home, one old motel renovated into several apartments, and the bakery.

The factory consisted of a basement, main production floor, and a second floor with a small apartment. The main building had been constructed in the 1800's and the side buildings in the 1900's. During a brief tour of the building, John learned more about the bakery's rich history. His guide explained that, in the early years, The Amana Society Bakery served only the village of South Amana. Each village in the Colonies had their own bakeries to supply bread to the families located there. Horse-drawn wagons delivered the baked goods, and as the driver approached a kitchen, he rang a bell. A woman from the kitchen heard the bell and came out to tell the driver how many loaves the kitchen needed, usually about a dozen. On Saturdays, the driver brought coffee cakes to serve on Sunday morning.

Adjacent to the factory, the owners had constructed a smaller wood building for the office. An enclosed hallway connected this wholesale and retail headquarters to the factory, allowing office personnel to walk between the two structures year-round, sheltered from the elements. John admired the design as both efficient and practical.

After the factory tour, John felt confident he could improve operations and grow the bakery. He described his experience with his own factory in Czechoslovakia, and his passion for the business. He had never produced bread. However, he was quick to learn and explore. Because of his intelligence and strong work ethic, he always started at the bottom and ended up at the top. The two men decided John would manage the bakery until he had the finances to purchase it. Without a written contract, a common practice in both Europe and the USA, they shook hands to seal the agreement. John would start work as soon as he had given notice to his other four jobs.

John drove through the area before he returned home to Jarmila with the good news. He told her about the bakery and the charming rural villages nestled into the rural setting. The job included living quarters above the bakery.

"You will love it, Jarmila. In the Amana Colonies, the houses are surrounded by wooded hills, lush farmland, and sparkling rivers. It reminds me of Trutnov, except there are no mountains."

He moved his family into the cluster of small villages that July, where John became the general manager of the Amana Society Bakery. It was 1955. He was 45 years old and ready to take on the challenge of building the small-town bakery into a regional business. At the time, he had no comprehension of how the move would affect Jarmila.

Although the beautiful natural surroundings were ideal for raising a family—and Jarmila loved the picturesque rural setting—she had difficulty getting acquainted with the residents there. Jarmila soon learned the small town was tight knit and conservative. The church conducted services for Amana natives only, in German—a language that had traumatized her since the Nazis had terrorized their homeland.

Jarmila was a sophisticated woman who appreciated orchestra concerts and ballet performances in a community that felt "entertainment" was unnecessary. She was beautiful and intelligent amidst the churchgoers who required women to cover their heads and remain in the background. She was 35 years old, the mother of five children, with a world of experience behind her, and she had no one to talk to. Except for the fact that she had children who were busy in their own lives, Jarmila had nothing in common with the women her age in Upper South Amana. After only a few months in Upper South Amana, Jarmila retreated further into herself and directed her attention to raising her children.

Jarmila was not fluent in English, but she spoke German. She had been raised Catholic. The closed culture of the Amana Colonies smothered her. She didn't drive, so she had no opportunity to meet new people or join in any activities. She was isolated. John was busy building the business and had very little time for anything else. They only had Sundays to spend time together.

John dove into the bakery with energy and enthusiasm. From the first day he arrived, John demonstrated his desire to succeed. He quickly earned the respect of his employees. Before the week was over, John had set the tone for a new management style. Soon, the business was humming with activity. John's employees liked him. He was friendly and fair, and he paid a good wage. The outgoing Czech, with his charming accent and sparkling blue eyes, greeted everyone with a smile.

Happy employees arrived at work early, only to discover their boss was there ahead of them. John was the first person to check in at the bakery, and the last to leave at night. His work ethic set an example for every employee. Most were farm women or small-town residents who worked to supplement their family income. They learned that he never asked more of them than he did of himself.

When John began his position as manager, the bakery sold bread to the restaurants in Amana and at a few small local towns and Cedar Rapids. In the months before John assumed control, the Amana line of breads accounted for $9,000 per month in sales volume. John set goals to improve the plant sanitation, product quality, variety, marketing and distribution. He wrote job descriptions for every position in the company.

"Sanitation is important to quality," John told them. "This machine is your responsibility. You must take care of it and keep it clean at all times. Plan your work schedule accordingly."

John made a habit of walking through the plant often. He lavished attention on those who kept their workspace sparkling clean and still accomplished their production quotas. He congratulated the already beaming employee for a job well done, then turned to his co-workers with the reminder: "This is how you do it!" Before long, every worker vied for John's attention. Most of the workers were clean, hardworking farm ladies who understood the need and were conscious of sanitary practices. They did a good job. If an employee fell short, John always spoke with the worker privately.

Soon, the workers became more efficient with their supplies. They reduced accidents and spillage. They increased productivity. John saw the results on the company's bottom line. After just three months on the job, John shared the news with Jarmila.

"We started at $9,000 per month in sales and have already climbed to $10,000 per month," he said.

Jarmila cocked her head. "And are you satisfied with that number?"

John leaned back in his chair and laughed. "You know me too well," he said. "This is just the beginning."

CHAPTER TWENTY-THREE

LEADING THE WAY

That same month, on September 25, 1955, the *Cedar Rapids Gazette* published an article about the irony of John's selection as the new manager for the bakery. Laurie Van Dyke, staff writer, told the story:

AMANA—A man imprisoned as a capitalist in his native Czechoslovakia has found his first satisfaction in America in this colony that turned down communal living in favor of capitalism.

John Honolka owned his own bakery in Trutnov, near the German Polish border. Then came the Communist revolution in 1948 and three days later the bakery was wrested from him. He was thrown into prison, labeled a capitalist.

Honolka is not quite the capitalist in America that he was in Czechoslovakia. he does not even own his own bakery yet. But he is the new manager of the Amana colonies bakery in Upper South Amana.

The new bakery manager has the initiative to become an American capitalist. Only a short time after his entry into the country in 1951, he had written to Chambers of Commerce all over the country about ways to get his bakery specialty, a German wafer, on the market.

The anomaly of having a Czech as manager of a bakery noted for its German products can be explained readily by the fact that Honolka lived in German Czechoslovakia. His bakery there produced fine German pastries.

"This is what I need," said Honolka after three months in his manager's job. "For the first time since I came to America I am very, very satisfied."

"For a young man to start over again in this country is quite easy. For an old man it's not so easy," said the 44-year-old Honolka.

"If only we had come here 20 years ago," concurred his blonde wife, who has just recently moved family belongings into the upper story of the bakery building. "There's a lot more opportunity here than over there."

Young at Heart

The appearance of both the Honolkas belies their talk about getting old. Their good humor is more in evidence than any regrets about the past.

Honolka does not waste time worrying about becoming a capitalist in this country. He has five children to feed and educate.

He would still like to get his German wafer, the Karlsbader, on the market, but the $2,000 the wafer machine would cost is too much to think about—he's more anxious to put his children through college.

Anything else is too far in the future.

"The main problem for me now is to give my children a good education and profession—that's all I want," said Honolka. "The main problem is to live as a free people in a free country."

The Honolka children are Eva, 18, Don, 16, Vlasta, 13, John, 9, and Tommy, 5.

They were all born in Czechoslovakia except Tommy, born while his parents were refugees in Germany, and his father was working for the French secret police.

Screened Refugees

It was Honolka's job then to help screen refugees in Germany, to determine whether they were Communist spies or actual political refugees. He worked in Germany from the time of his escape in 1948 until his immigration to the United States in 1951.

Honolka spent three months in a forced labor camp in the coal mines before he managed the escape of himself and his family through the aid of a friend. The camp contained persons who had been businessmen and factory owners.

"They arrested me because they said, as they say for everybody: 'He is a capitalist,'" the Czech recalled.

The family's sponsor in this country was a Czech farmer. Honolka worked on a farm for a short time and then moved to Cedar Rapids. He could not find a job in a bakery, so he worked for a sausage factory, since closed. Then he went to work in the meat department of Daniels Park Foods, where he worked until he became manager of the Amana bakery three months ago. The bakery is owned by the Amana Society.

Hard Worker

Honolka worked up from the bottom to become owner of the bakery in his native land. The work was hard even after he was head man. Sometimes he worked from 3 in the morning until 10 at night.

Days are not so long for him here, though he is on the job seven days a week. The bakery has a staff of about 25 persons. The number increased somewhat since Honolka became manager.

He already has added two new products to the bakery's line, a new type of coffee cake and an all-rye bread. He hopes to add more products in the future.

A third bakery route to Davenport is to be added soon. Routes now are to Marshalltown and Newton, and to Iowa City, Cedar Rapids and Manchester. In addition, there are special deliveries for all the Amana Colonies.

Speaks Four Languages

When the Honolkas came to Cedar Rapids, they could speak little English, and they sought friends who could speak their language. This could have been any one of several languages, since Honolka speaks Czech, German, Polish and French.

Someone told him to visit the Amanas. There were Germans there, he was told, who would talk German with them.

Honolka followed the suggestion, and the family soon had friends in Amana, one of them Fred Geiger, manager of the general store in Main Amana. It was Geiger who told Honolka about the manager's job at the colony bakery and was instrumental in bringing him to Amana.

The upper story of the bakery building, red brick like most colony structures, was remodeled at one end into an apartment. The Honolkas moved in three weeks ago and the children began attending class at the school in Middle Amana.

The school bus stops in front of the bakery each morning. The four older children were St. Wenceslaus students in Cedar Rapids last year when the family lived at 1507 Hamilton Street SW, Cedar Rapids, Iowa.

After school and on weekends, the older children help in the bakery, and Eva is head salesgirl on Saturdays.

Eva already has plans for her college education. Then there will be four more children to educate…a task that would challenge even a capitalist.

While John guided his employees in new ways to improve the bakery, Jarmila spent her time with the two youngest children, Honzik (Johnny) and Tommy.

Eva, 18, participated on the cheerleading squad in Amana, where Lada, 16, excelled at nearly every sport. That fall, he attended classes, stayed after school for basketball practice, arrived home in time to eat dinner, and spent his evenings helping at the bakery. Vlasta, 13, rode the bus to school in the morning, and back again in the afternoon. She worked at the bakery after school and on Saturdays. All the older children learned to perform any tasks they were assigned— from sweeping the floors to applying price labels on packaged bread.

Among the most popular products at the time were the "Butter Horns," best sellers also known as "croissants." Vlasta made thousands of them every day. She spread fifty-pound blocks of butter between thin layers of floured dough, repeating this roll-and-butter process three times before sliding them onto a tray and into a freezer to harden. The fourth time she rolled the dough thin, then sliced it and formed it into croissant shapes on large baking sheets and slid them into a "proof box" where the steam caused the dough to rise more quickly. Finally, the rolls went into the oven to bake. The result was delicious: a rich, fluffy, crispy roll. No matter how many croissants Vlasta baked, there were never enough to meet the demand.

Life in the Amana Colonies was a boy's paradise for Johnny, 9, and

Tommy, 5. After Johnny left on the bus for school in the morning, Jarmila and Tommy explored the fields and streams around them. She sometimes packed a picnic lunch and walked with her youngest son through the wooded area behind the bakery. After school and on weekends, Johnny and Tommy swam in nearby ponds and fished on the Cedar River. Jarmila encouraged them to enjoy nature. They built huts made from fallen branches of the trees and spent countless hours playing cowboys and Indians.

Often, Jarmila carried a sewing project outside, where she could watch the boys play while she crocheted a dresser scarf or embroidered a set of tea towels, napkins and a tablecloth. An accomplished seamstress, she found comfort in every stitch. Though Jarmila had few friends her own age, her home became a popular gathering place for her children's school friends. Lada's high school buddies often appeared on her doorstep around mealtime. Jarmila always found a way to feed them. The teenage boys loved her cooking, and she loved to watch them eat.

That fall, Eva entered the Miss Iowa pageant. It was only the third year for the event, started in 1952 as part of the Miss USA competition. Eva managed to fit rehearsals for the pageants into her already busy life without missing a beat. She had a little money saved and bought inexpensive clothes and a bathing suit for the competition. Eva was self-conscious and knew her chances of winning were low. She was excited to place second in the pageant. Eva's success did not surprise John and Jarmila. They were used to seeing their oldest daughter excel.

All the Honolka children had learned to work hard for their accomplishments. After just four years in America, they still remembered their days in the refugee camps. They viewed both their schoolwork and their jobs as privileges in the land of freedom.

CHAPTER TWENTY-FOUR

GROWING THE BAKERY

Temperatures hit freezing levels in early December 1955. Heavy snow fell, and John Jr. and Tommy spent their free time playing outdoors, sledding down the steep hills around Upper South Amana. Jarmila bundled them into warm coats and scarves for their adventures.

"The season is still cold and dark. But when I watch the children play, things seem a little brighter," Jarmila said. "If only they could stay small for a little while longer. Babies grow up too fast."

Tommy liked school and was a good student. One evening at suppertime, he informed the family of his second-grade field trip by bus to the Amana Refrigeration Plant a short distance from school. At the end of the tour, the guide showed them a metal box and told them the box would revolutionize cooking. It was called a Radar Range. (Later, Amana introduced America's first countertop microwave. It was called the Amana Radarange, which debuted in 1967 and sold for $495.)

John heard from a friend that Frank Newman planned to enlist in OCS— Officer Candidate School in the US Army. The two had lost contact in recent years. John was happy to hear that Frank had found a place in the military, and in the U.S. He invited Frank to spend Christmas with the Honolkas in South Amana. Frank eagerly agreed. It had been over four years since he had talked with his old friend from the refugee camps.

John welcomed Frank with a firm handshake when he arrived.

"You look good, Frank."

"Thank you, John. So do you. The last time I saw you, we were hungry and tired. Life in America has changed us for the better."

John described his family's journey to the U.S. and his new job at the Amana Bakery. "I am finally where I belong," he said.

Frank told how he had enlisted in the U.S. Army in 1952, while he was still in displaced persons status. "Earlier this year, I was assigned a position as an aide to Major General Bolling. the Theater Commander. Apparently, he saw some potential others didn't," Frank said.

As a non-United States citizen, Frank could not qualify for Officer Candidate School (OCS) without a waiver from the Army High Command. General Boling recognized Frank's leadership qualities, his education, his deportment and bearing—and placed his full weight behind the waiver. "Now I will become an officer," Frank said.

"Congratulations! This will open new doors for you," John said. "I've always believed you would accomplish great things."

Jarmila was also happy to see Frank. He was a Czech, so she could speak her native language with him and exchange poetry. Often, they shared jokes and riddles. Frank was good natured, polite and distinguished. Jarmila could easily converse with him. She had missed that kind of conversation and was eager to visit with Frank.

While he was in town, Frank took time to visit with each of the children, but it was Eva that caught his attention. She listened to his story of enlisting in the U.S. Army with interest. Then, she described her life as a teenager in the Amanas.

"I go to high school," she said. "When I graduate, I want to attend the Art Institute in Chicago. I have a scholarship."

Frank admired one of the paintings Eva had brought home from school. "You have talent," he said.

Later, Jarmila and Eva prepared dinner, and the family gathered around the table. Throughout the meal, Frank couldn't take his eyes off Eva. The frail little girl had turned into a beautiful teenager. He learned she was a cheerleader for her school, worked in the bakery, and dreamed of being an artist.

For Frank, it was love at first sight.

With plenty of good food and laughter, the evening passed quickly. Frank turned to John after Eva left the room. "Is this the same child who was too shy to speak to me at the camps?"

"She's a young woman already," John said.

Frank decided to be straightforward with his friend. "I'm twenty-eight, and I'm in love with your daughter," he said. "I'd like your permission to marry her."

John had noticed Frank's obvious interest in Eva. While it had been years since the two had seen each other, they still had a strong bond from their shared experiences at the refugee camps. John admired and respected the young man who sat across from him. He didn't hesitate.

"It may take some time for her to get used to the idea."

"I'll win her over, sir."

During the few days he stayed with the Honolkas, Frank spent time with Eva. They talked about life in America and their plans for the future. He learned she spoke fluent English. She told him more of her dreams of becoming an artist. But she was still in high school—not thinking of a serious relationship.

The spring of 1956, John took steps to expand the bakery's business by reaching out to major markets within a reasonable driving distance. He traveled to Des Moines and arranged to have fresh bread delivered there three days a week. It was a direct route on Highway 6, straight west. John figured if his delivery truck left at 3 a.m., the bread would arrive before 8 a.m. Along the way, the driver also delivered to Marengo, Grinnell, Newton, and other small towns. He completed the route and returned to the bakery by 5 or 6 p.m.

The additional sales more than paid for the expense of the driver. To enhance his volume, John developed a larger selection of breads and rolls. Soon, he offered round white, stone ground, caraway rye, farm bread, sourdough, French bread, Vienna bread, potato rolls, and of course butter horns. John created each new recipe from scratch.

That same year, John's friend, Bill Zuber, who owned a restaurant in Homestead (the seventh Amana Colony), approached John about helping him with a popular pickled ham meal the restaurant served. The large hams required large ovens. Bill would bring the hams to the bakery, and John would wrap them in bread dough and bake them in the large bread ovens. Bill had been a major league pitcher for the New York Yankees. He and John often discussed sports and business. They had much in common and became good friends.

John was always adding products to his offerings at the bakery. Nearly every week, he experimented with something new. When a fresh batch of rolls or a new variety of bread came out of the oven, he carried it to their upstairs living quarters. Jarmila and their children were accustomed to seeing John walk through the door in his white baker's uniform with something in his hands.

"Who wants to taste something delicious?" John set his latest bread flavor on the kitchen table.

His family delighted in serving as his taste-testers. They took their job seriously, and John valued their feedback. He encouraged them to provide honest opinions, which often led to disagreements.

Afterwards, John tweaked the recipe. He produced a two-gallon batch of dough and tested it on others. Sometimes, he offered a new variety to a nearby restaurant, where the public could weigh-in on the flavor. This form of market research guided most of John's new product development. Soon, his product line offered 20 different varieties of breads and rolls. The new markets, combined with added products, resulted in increased sales and profits. John expanded the staff to produce the volume required.

As the bakery thrived, the Honolka family became more immersed in the Amana community. The children did well in school. Jarmila spent most of her time at home, cooking, cleaning and sewing. When the spring weather arrived, Jarmila took long walks in the woods or sometimes swam in the pond where wildlife roamed. She picked wildflowers and weeds and fashioned them into beautiful bouquets for the kitchen table.

It was still early in 1956 when John went to the bank to make arrangements to purchase the bakery. Eva went with her father to the bank.

Sitting across from the loan officer, John described his successful business in Czechoslovakia. "We supported 25 employees, before the Communists confiscated the bakery."

Impressed by John's obvious passion for growing a business, the banker listened to John's plans for the Amana Society Bakery. Eva perched on the other chair beside her father, translating a word or two, when he faltered with his English.

After a half-hour conversation, the loan officer shook his head. "I can see why you succeeded in your own country, Mr. Honolka. You had an engaging personality and the support of family and friends. But you have no collateral."

"We have already improved the profits of the bakery," John said. "And we have plans to expand the product line and our distribution."

"To loan you money, our bank would require collateral."

John turned to Eva for a translation. "He means you have to show a way to pay them back if the bakery fails."

"I will not fail," John said. "Look at my daughter, Eva. I have five children who will work with me to guarantee we can pay you back."

The banker turned down John's request.

The news was a disappointment, but John was not deterred. He believed he could find a way to buy the business. First, he would prove his competence by increasing sales and profits.

The Amana Society Bakery with delivery trucks, when John Honolka grew the business in the 1950s.

CHAPTER TWENTY-FIVE

EVA GETS MARRIED

In May 1956, Eva turned 19. She planned to graduate from high school, work full time at the bakery that summer, and enroll in the Chicago Art Institute in the fall—though her scholarship offer had not yet arrived.

John watched Eva race to the mailbox each day. Privately, he told Jarmila he hoped the scholarship would not materialize.

"We cannot allow her to go to Chicago," John said.

"You'll break her heart."

"She will recover."

In June, Eva received the long-awaited letter: The Chicago Art Institute offered her a full scholarship. Eva shared the scholarship news with her parents.

"I'm in! Now I can go to Chicago and study art."

John shook his head. "No."

"But this is what I want to do."

"Chicago is no place for a single girl to live," John said. "A young woman of 19, living by herself in Chicago? The city is full of Mafia! That will not happen. It isn't safe. You will go to Texas and marry Frank Newman."

The news shocked Eva. "I barely know him," she said.

"I know him," her father replied. "He's a good Czech, and an honorable man. He will take good care of you."

"But I don't love him."

"Love is not everything you need for a marriage," John said. "Frank understands you. He was with us six years ago in the refugee camps. He knows what you have sacrificed for freedom."

Eva's parents raised her to honor them. She was too obedient to defy her father. Instead, she went to Cedar Rapids to shop for a wedding gown.

On the Fourth of July 1956, her father put her on an airplane and sent her to Austin, Texas, to marry Frank Charles Newman. Eva pleaded with her mother before she boarded the plane.

"I don't want to get married, Mom."

"Eva, if you marry out of love, you have thick glasses on your eyes," Jarmila told her. "You do not see reality. And sometimes when you take them off and you do see reality, it's not all gold that glitters."

She boarded the plane with one suitcase, a full-length white-lace wedding gown, and $5 in her pocketbook. Instead of heading to college, Eva was a frightened young woman, alone on a plane, headed out to marry a man she did not know. She did what any young woman would do in a similar situation: she cried.

Frank met her at the airport and drove past the Catholic Church so she could see where their wedding would take place.

The morning of their wedding, Frank brought Eva a bouquet to match the blossom details of her wedding gown. They married on July 5, 1956.

The officer's club hosted a reception, and the happy couple ate sardines for their wedding dinner. It was all they could afford.

Afterward, they went back to their apartment. Eva was terrified. Frank took her hand and led her to the bedroom. "You will sleep here," he said. "I will sleep on the couch until you learn to love me."

For the next three months, Frank courted Eva. He took her out for dinner and to the movies. They went dancing, took long walks together, and shared their dreams for the future. Frank taught Eva how to drive a car—something she had never learned because her father had not believed that ladies should drive. John felt women should be driven wherever they needed to go.

Before she married Frank, all Eva knew of military officers was what she remembered from the horror of German soldiers who wore uniforms. And now, her husband wore a uniform. As she watched him go through officer's training, Eva learned to appreciate the structure of the military. She observed the U.S. Army's commitment to serving families, and to guarding their nation—instead of destroying their nation, as the Nazis had done.

Soon, Eva learned to love the man she had married, and the military life he had chosen. Frank's patience paid off: Eva was pregnant. Upon graduation from Officer Candidate School, Frank was commissioned a 2nd Lieutenant of Artillery in the U.S. Army. He entered Army flight training and earned his wings in December 1956. He and Eva talked about what this would mean for their family.

"I love to fly," Frank said. "But this assignment is likely to take me away from you for long stretches of time. Army pilots go where they are needed most."

"General Bolling said you were born to fly." Eva touched the wings pinned to his uniform. You will succeed at anything you do."

When 2nd Lieutenant Newman received orders to ship out to Korea for 18 months, Eva returned home to live with her parents in Iowa. She wasn't thrilled about the move, but Frank insisted.

"Eva, I don't want you here in Texas, alone," he said.

She cried. "I don't want to go back. I'll have to work in the bakery again!"

Every day he was away, Eva raced to the mailbox in Iowa, just as she had a year earlier when she waited for word on her art scholarship. But this time, she watched for letters from Frank. She was never disappointed. Her husband wrote each day the entire time he was away.

Eva spent the winter months adjusting to her new status. Eva was happy to be in Upper South Amana, with her own mother, while she waited for the birth of her first child.

Jarmila and Eva had always been close; Eva's pregnancy brought them even closer. They worked side-by-side to do the household chores, and supervised Johnny and Tom. Johnny was in charge of his younger brother; Tommy followed him everywhere. They swam, fished and hunted bullfrogs at the South Amana Pond and fished in the Iowa River.

The boys rode their bikes along the country roads and hunted in the fields and forests. They had BB guns and shot at most everything, including at each other. Together, they chased after birds, dogs, cats, and squirrels. They aimed at targets tacked to hay bales, broken windows in old sheds, and assorted glass bottles they lined upon fence rails or rocks. They made bombs out of M-80 firecrackers.

One afternoon, Jarmila looked out the window and saw her sons racing across the field toward home. They slammed into the kitchen, clamoring to tell of their latest adventure. Sweat poured down their faces. Both boys struggled to catch their breath. Johnny's jeans were ripped at the knees. Tommy's hair and eyes were filled with dirt; the palms of his hands scratched.

"Slow down," Jarmila said. "Now take a deep breath and tell us what happened."

Tommy threw his hands in the air. His eyes shone with excitement. "Johnny shot a bull in the nuts, and he came after us."

"He was real mad," Johnny said. "We had to get outta there," Tommy added.

Jarmila choked back her smile while the boys told their story. Gently, she explained to her sons that what they did to the bull was unkind and wrong. "Animals have feelings just like you," she said. "How would you feel if someone did this to you?"

The boys took the lesson to heart. From that point forward, they loved and respected animals. Johnny loved them all and brought a variety of injured animals home for Jarmila to heal. One afternoon, they climbed the metal stairway and traipsed into the kitchen carrying a cardboard box. Johnny set it on the table in the center of the room, where Eva sat, peeling carrots.

"Guess what we have!" Tommy couldn't wait to share their discovery with his big sister.

"Is it alive?" Eva knew her brothers had a history of capturing turtles and frogs, which they dragged into the house—only to have Jarmila send them outside where they belonged or nurse them back to health.

"Yes," Tommy said, "Wanna see?"

"Does it bite?" Eva moved her batch of carrots to the sink before she approached the box.

"Maybe," Tommy said.

"It's not poisonous," John Jr. added.

Eva opened the lid to see one small pigeon nestled into the corner. The bird had a broken leg. "This is a baby, Tommy. Where'd you find him?"

"Over by Mr. Kellenberger's shed. Pat said we could keep him." Pat Kellenberger was Tommy's age. The family lived next door.

Eva shook her head. "I don't know, boys. Mom might not want birds living in the house."

After Jarmila taped the bird's leg to a splint, it wasn't long before the pigeon hopped around like new. Johnny and Tom tried their best to convince Jarmila the pigeon would be a perfect pet. In the end, Jarmila relented. They named him Pepee and allowed him to live in the attic, where he could fly out the window and perch on the roof of the bakery. The boys played with the pigeon every afternoon for the next few weeks—feeding him corn seed and worms as treats. Most of the time, Jarmila took care of the pigeon, who became domesticated and everyone's pet.

Another school year had begun. Lada—who had Americanized his name to Don, to better fit in with his classmates—played several sports, lettering in each of them. Vlasta was tired of people mispronouncing her name, so she found a translation and changed it to Patricia. John Jr. was the rambunctious one.

Now in the fourth grade, Johnny thrived in the outdoors. He rode his bicycle to the West Amana dam and fished for carp, crappie, bullhead, catfish and pike. He hunted rabbits, pheasants, and ground squirrels. Wherever he went, little Tommy trailed behind him. The two boys were inseparable. When John Jr. and Tommy weren't getting into mischief outside, they spent time in the bakery. John gave them jobs to do and paid them a few dollars. Late in the day, they showed up in Jarmila's kitchen, covered head-to-toe in flour.

The bakery continued to exceed John's projections. He extended the delivery route to include independent distributors in Omaha and Lincoln, Nebraska, who would deliver to retail stores. The distance was nearly 300 miles, but, once again, the increased volume more than paid for the delivery cost. The new markets—combined with a broader product line—resulted in significant gains. Soon, the sales hit $18,000 per month—double what it was when John took over the bakery, and far surpassing the Amana Society's wildest dreams.

As the demand for his products grew, John researched new production methods and more efficient systems. In the building's basement they stored 100-pound bags of flour, along with a flour hopper and a huge boiler for hot water. There was enough space for a full truckload of 800 flour bags, which were manually unloaded by sliding the bags out of the truck, down a wooden ramp into the basement and hand stacked. It was a labor-intensive process. To move the flour upstairs, the flour hopper cork-screwed flour up into the main production area, to two bread mixers that mixed all the ingredients into a dough.

The main production floor contained a large professional mixer, a roll machine, a divider, rounder, overhead proofer, sheeter, proof box, and three ovens. Another area held wheeled wire cooling racks, various bread pans, and a large washing station where workers cleaned the bread pans after use.

John's manufacturing processes maximized efficiency throughout the bakery. A separate building housed production areas for the bread to be cooled, sliced, bagged and placed onto wire racks, ready to load into delivery trucks for the local Iowa markets. This is also where some products were boxed and placed into a freezer for transport to distant markets. The distributors for those markets picked up the frozen bread in the afternoon. The bread thawed during the overnight journey to their destination, arriving fresh for distribution the following day.

A typical production day began at 4:30 a.m., in the mixing room, where bakers would process between 16 and 34 batches of dough a day, each weighing approximately 250-350 pounds. The dough would go through the mixer, a divider, a rounder, an overhead proofer, and a sheeter before being panned, proofed, baked, removed from the pans, cooled, sliced and bagged. John insisted on sanitary conditions, which required the workers to clean their equipment as they worked. Workers always waxed the bakery's wooden floors daily, and every employee learned how to use both dry and wet mops. When the production shift concluded, everyone cleaned their stations again. Around 4 p.m., the bakers turned off the gas ovens; at 6 p.m., they loaded the delivery trucks.

But there was still work to be done. At the end of each day, the workers mixed night sponges for up to eight batches of bread dough, to allow for fermentation overnight. And, although the bakery became silent around 8 p.m., someone had to turn the ovens back on around midnight; to assure they would reach the correct baking temperature for the next day.

John trained his children to perform all the tasks they could safely handle. Each of them began to help at the bakery at an early age, placing pricing stickers on plastic bags, and sweeping the floors. Over time, they learned to run the mixers, dividers, sheeters, proof boxes, slicers, ovens, and flour bins. They mixed ingredients, handled night sponges, and Don drove bread routes. They developed strong work ethics that would serve them well in their future careers.

That winter, the family applied to become naturalized American citizens. John, Jarmila and Eva took classes on citizenship in anticipation of the big event. They had to live in the country for at least five years, before they could apply to become U.S. citizens. The time had finally arrived.

Children over the age of 16—like Eva—were required to apply, just as John and Jarmila did. Upon their parents' approval, the younger children automatically received citizenship. John, Jarmila, and Eva completed their forms, took their naturalization test, and paid the fee.

The FBI had already fingerprinted and investigated them. The written test and formal interview were the final requirements. Since Eva had just returned to Iowa, she couldn't complete the test until she had lived there at least three months. To accommodate her schedule and meet all the requirements, they planned to complete their process after the birth of her baby in April. Eva was nervous before her interview.

"What if I don't remember the answer to a question?"

"You will remember," John said. "We know more about U.S. history and government than most Americans.

"I can't believe it's finally happening. After all that we gave for freedom, my child will be born in America—a U.S. citizen with all the rights and privileges we fought to achieve."

Tears sparkled in the corners of Jarmila's eyes. "We must always be proud of both—the country of our birth, and the country that gave us our freedom."

After the Christmas holidays, Eva's baby grew more active inside her. She had gained little weight, but she tired easily. In late March, two weeks before her due date, Eva prayed that God would give her strength and wisdom. A sense of calm settled around her.

"I can't wait to hold my baby," Eva told Jarmila.

The day before her due date, Eva slept late. She woke to the sun streaming onto her pillow. Her contractions began after breakfast. Jarmila gave her daughter hot tea and instructed her to walk around the kitchen.

"Let me know when your pains are ten minutes apart," she said.

"The baby is healthy and active," Eva said. "Kicking and turning all the time."

"He's going to be a beautiful baby boy," Jarmila said.

Eva laughed at her mother's certainty. "How do you know that?"

"Easy. You sleep on your left side, and you're carrying this baby low and forward." Jarmila placed her hand lightly on Eva's belly. "Just like I did with your brothers."

"Mom, those are myths," Eva said.

By evening, Eva's contractions were faster and harder. John and Jarmila drove her to the Marengo hospital. Her labor continued to intensify through the night. At dawn, Eva's doctor spoke privately to John and Jarmila. "She's a small woman, and we expected this to be a difficult delivery. But Eva is determined. It won't be long now."

The long-awaited baby arrived quietly on Saturday, April 6, 1957. The kind doctor laid Eva's baby boy in her arms. She named her son, Michael Frank Newman. He died at birth. The cord wrapped around his tiny neck five times.

Eva was 20, and alone, but her faith grew stronger. She insisted on a proper burial for the baby. She had seen too many infants carried out of the Hungarian prison in brown paper bags. Her family attended the funeral in Marengo, Iowa.

On the day of the service, Eva quoted the scripture that spoke to her. "Do you not know, can you not see, that from dust you were made and to dust you shall return, but my soul and spirit will rise again."

On April 9, 1957, three days after baby Michael Frank Newman died at birth, Eva and her family became Naturalized Citizens of the United States of America. As Eva pledged her allegiance to the American flag, tears filled her eyes and ran down her cheeks.

Lt. Col. Frank Newman never saw his firstborn son. Eva never got over the perfectly shaped, beautiful baby boy, her first born. Over the years, she shed tears many times remembering her sweet infant.

CHAPTER TWENTY-SIX

CHANGE IS IN THE AIR

1957-58

Eva stayed with her parents while Frank completed his assignment in Korea. Though she counted the days until Frank's return, Eva found a new joy in watching her siblings grow. After losing her own child, she understood why Jarmila had always wanted to keep her family close. The two women—mother and daughter—spent much of the summer together.

That June, Don turned 17. He recruited several of his friends to work at the bakery. When they arrived promptly at 8 a.m., John was there to welcome them.

"You're late," he said.

"But Don said to be here at eight," one teenager replied.

Don recited the mantra he had often heard from his father: "If you aren't fifteen minutes early to an appointment or a job, you're late."

In the end, the starting time for the job didn't matter. The work was too hard for Don's friends. After a day of unloading 100-pound bags of flour from a truck like Don did, they quit.

Don had the same work ethic as his father. He was organized and confident. Honest and self-motivated. Don made no excuses; he was his own worst critic when he fell short of his goals—which rarely happened. John was proud of his son. "You work all summer in the bakery, and you will have money for your first car, plus insurance," John said. Before school started that fall, Don bought his car, a 1939 Ford.

Johnny admired his brother's car but was too young to drive. One evening after work, Don walked outside to get into his car and discovered the right side of the vehicle had totally caved in. Little Johnny, age 10, had taken the car for a ride and hit a fire hydrant. The cost to repair the damage was greater than the value of the car. Don bought another to replace it. This time, he chose a black 1945 Ford Club Coupe, which he also purchased with money he earned himself.

Vlasta, now going by her American name of Patricia, was 14. She worked in the bakery every day after school, on Saturdays, and full time in the summers, earning money for her school clothes, shoes, lunches, school supplies, and activities. Without transportation, she only participated in the activities where she could take the school bus or depend on friends to provide a ride.

She learned to operate all the bakery equipment and worked wherever she was needed. Patricia also made butter horns, streusel coffee cakes, cookies, and potato rolls. The bakery was so successful it became a popular stop for tour buses. The fragrance of fresh-baked bread drew visitors, but the sheer volume of products often overwhelmed them. Tourists stood wide-eyed, with astonished expressions on their faces, as they moved from one machine to the next and asked dozens of questions. Tour guides had their hands full, keeping to their allotted time.

In August 1957, American Bandstand premiered on national television. Slinkys and Hula Hoops were popular throughout the U.S. The Soviet Union successfully conducted a long-range test flight of the first intercontinental ballistic missile. Jarmila read the news and remembered the unpleasant Russian Communists, a reminder she didn't need. Though she harbored negative memories of the Russian soldiers, Jarmila understood the Russian people also suffered under their own leaders and invaders. She had read about the Battle of Stalingrad and was knowledgeable about world affairs.

That September, Civil Rights issues raised their ugly head in America. President Dwight D. Eisenhower sent 101st Airborne Division troops to Little Rock, Arkansas, to enforce desegregation laws at Central High School. Meanwhile, Frank Newman returned home to his wife. He and Eva began their military life in Boston, Massachusetts.

Without Eva, Jarmila felt alone again. Don and Patricia were constantly away from home, working with their father or attending school functions. Don was at the bakery at 3 a.m. to run a bakery route before he went to class each day. John traveled on sales calls for the business several days a week. This left Jarmila with John Jr. and Tommy, who grew more independent each day. Although she occupied herself with long walks in the woods and an occasional swim in the South Amana Pond during the summer, Jarmila rarely left the house in the fall and winter. She cooked alone, cleaned alone, and spent her spare time in solitary pursuits like sewing, reading, crocheting or embroidery.

The family had no telephone except the one in the bakery office. And without transportation, Jarmila could not socialize with anyone. John tried to teach her to drive on the country roads that surrounded the bakery, but Jarmila did poorly. She had seen too many bad accidents on the evening news and feared she might cause one.

Normally, Jarmila was a social person. She enjoyed being around others. She had a good sense of humor, enjoyed laughing, and was tolerant and kind toward everyone. But the isolation of her life took a toll on Jarmila, sending her into depression. She was still pleasant, but she had lost her happy spirit. John saw a change in his wife but was helpless to do anything about it. Even Johnny and Tommy noticed their mother was quieter than usual. They entertained Jarmila with stories they brought home from school, but she seemed preoccupied and distant.

When the holidays arrived, Jarmila hadn't improved. John focused his attention on the one thing he controlled: the bakery. He expanded the distribution routes into another state. Sales multiplied and John again asked to buy the bakery. Ironically, John's meteoric success with the bakery worked against him. With each improvement he made, profits increased. The Amana Society had decided the bakery was now not for sale. They weren't interested in purchasing costly new equipment; they were content to have John manage the bakery for them at the current level.

Something had to change.

John and Jarmila had talked about a move to California for four years. Now, after 2 ½ years in South Amana, John felt frustrated. He could not purchase the bakery, and the owners didn't share his vision for growth. Their children were growing up and moving away. Jarmila was unhappy in the small village. The Upper South Amana colony consisted only of the bakery, a barn, an old small hotel converted to two apartments, three brick Amana homes, and one new ranch-style house. John and Jarmila and their children lived above the bakery, where the attic had been made into an apartment. From all accounts, Southern California was the place to be. It was the land of dreams, with Hollywood and the Pacific Ocean. Sunshine and prosperity called to John and Jarmila, and they responded.

In March 1958, John quit his job at the bakery, packed Jarmila and the two youngest boys into their car, and drove to Pasadena, California. John Jr. was 11, and Tommy was 8. The trip took six long days of driving, through snowstorms in the mountain and a sandstorm in the New Mexico deserts— over 1,800 miles.

Don, 18, and Patricia, 15, stayed behind to finish the school year in Amana. They planned to join their parents by train that summer. But, by June, Don had an opportunity for a scholarship to become an athletics coach and didn't want to leave Iowa. Patricia, out of school, traveled to California, but her arrival wasn't enough to soothe Jarmila's melancholy.

After less than 90 days on the west coast, John and Jarmila abandoned the land of sun and fun. The beautiful California weather had not helped Jarmila's spirits. She was so depressed John was afraid to leave her alone. They returned to Cedar Rapids, Iowa in July, where John accepted a position with a company that owned four bakeries. He managed one of them.

That December, only nine months after he resigned from the South Amana bakery, the Amanas found John once again. Business had declined without him. They asked him to return to his former position. John wrote to his mother with the news:

John returned to the bakery after the Christmas break. In time, Jarmila
found solace in the beautiful countryside. She resumed her long walks and
her health improved. She was also now on antidepressants.

Once again, The Upper South Amana Bakery grew under John's
leadership. Soon, they delivered bread to a five-state region. The expanded
geographic area brought new challenges. Before 1928, bakeries across the
United States only sold bread in fresh, unwrapped loaves. People went to the
bakery to purchase their bread; they carried it home wrapped in paper or
tucked in a basket alongside their fresh fruits and vegetables from the
produce market.

Then, a man named Otto Frederick Rodwedder—a jeweler and inventor
born in Davenport, Iowa, about an hour and a half east of where an
entrepreneurial Czechoslovakian named John Honolka would one day make
his own improvements to the product—invented a machine to slice and wrap
bread. Rodwedder sold the machine to a Missouri-based baking company,
where they soon advertised:

'SLICED BREAD IS MADE HERE'

The company packaged the bread in a cardboard tin, to keep them fresh
longer. They included instructions for the consumer to: "Open the wrapper at
one end and pull out the pin" to access a slice of bread.[xxx]

From the 1930s, when John first became interested in baking, bakers
wrapped fresh loaves in wax paper. Workers heated the ends of the paper with

a hot iron rod to melt the wax and seal the paper. Later, they used cellophane paper and sealed the folded-over ends with glued-on labels. This kept the bread fresh until opened, but it was not easy to reseal afterward. Although some bread was now sold as whole loaves and others were sliced, the exterior wrapping hadn't changed much in 25 years.[xxxi] Each day, the Upper South Amana Bakery wrapped their fresh bread in paper or waxed paper for shipping. When John realized the paper cracked and bread dried out rapidly, he searched for a solution.

"My customers need fresh, soft bread. If the paper is cracked, parts of the loaf will be hard," he told Jarmila. "I need a better packaging process."

He found the answer in a new product—polyethylene. Originally invented in 1953 as a film called High-density Polyethylene (HDPE), the product was so new that manufacturers hadn't developed practical ways to use it. Then, Karl Ziegler of the Kaiser Wilhelm Institute and Erhard Holzkamp solved that problem. They realized the film could be closed, opened and re-closed easily with a twist tie. HDPE gave plastic film the quality it needed to be light and moldable, but still strong.[xxxii]

John Honolka was delighted with the solution. He was the first baker in the country to package bread in plastic bags. Like most visionaries, John didn't see his decision as a risk. He was confident the public would embrace the new "bagged bread." The modernization of his packaging process assured Amana bread would be fresh when customers purchased it – and remain fresh when they resealed the loaf day-after-day.

For Patricia, one of the most time-consuming jobs was bagging hundreds of loaves of bread into the new plastic bags—a process that could take hours each day. Still, she was grateful they no longer had to use the heated rod to seal the ends of waxed paper, as the bakery had packaged bread before the bags were invented.

True to his entrepreneurial spirit, John quickly parlayed the new bags into a marketing asset. Before long, he imprinted the bags with attractive logos, marketing messages, and content information. His sales increased. The profits soared.

Don watched his father's innovations and learned from them. Although he still intended to become a coach one day, he absorbed the business knowledge from his father. He learned all about manufacturing, distribution, marketing and sales—simply by watching John and working for the bakery. The skills would serve him well, as an adult.

By the spring of 1959, across America, people felt a growing sense that change was on the horizon. The birth of the microchip opened hundreds of possibilities for technological advancement. Researchers announced plans to introduce a new "birth control" pill that would change the lives of women everywhere. The Guggenheim Museum opened in New York with an entire collection of abstract "modern art."

For Jarmila, the change that mattered most was one in her own family: Eva had written she and Frank were expecting another baby. This time, her pregnancy went well. On June 14, 1959—Flag Day in America—Eva and Frank welcomed a healthy baby boy into the world. Their son, Michael, was born in Fort Devens, Massachusetts, where Frank was stationed. Like her mother before her, Eva had always wanted to have several children. Michael was the joy of her life.

With Frank home beside her, Eva quickly adapted to the army lifestyle. The young couple made lifelong friends, and Eva understood the pull of camaraderie the soldiers felt for each other. The U.S. Army became a second family. Their time at Fort Devens was brief. In 1960, Frank qualified to fly helicopters, just as the army began contemplating the formation of an "Air Cavalry" division—and five years before the Department of Defense funded the full program. Convinced the military could benefit from the superior mobility helicopters provided, army planners saw Frank as an integral part of their helicopter team. They transferred him to Germany. This time, he was assigned to the 14th Armored Cavalry Regiment.

CHAPTER TWENTY-SEVEN

LIFE IN THE SIXTIES

While Frank and Eva settled into their life in Germany, John and Jarmila had their hands full with John Jr. and Tommy. That summer, the boys—who loved exploring outdoors—tramped through the fields and forests, camped out, built fires, fished, and rode their bicycles everywhere. They made forts out of cornstalks in the middle of cornfields, built huts in the timber out of fallen branches, and sang songs at the top of their voices.

Johnny had a Philco transistor radio they listened to for hours. Rock and roll took off, and AM stations played Top 40 hits. He and Tommy preferred the "battle tunes." They knew all the words to *The Battle of New Orleans* and *Sink the Bismarck*. But their favorite was *Please Mr. Custer*. Tommy had a flair for the dramatic. He developed his own choreography for the song.

Please Mr. Custer, I don't wanna go
Hey, Mr. Custer, please don't make me go
I had a dream last night about the comin' fight
Somebody yelled "attack!"
And there I stood with an arrow in my back

Amana consisted of seven small villages, clustered together. The school was in Middle Amana. At 14, Johnny went to Amana High School, where he became a multiyear letterman in basketball and baseball. He was popular, good-hearted, a talented athlete, and a decent student. However, Johnny was also fun-loving and imaginative. As a result, he got into trouble with cars more times than the rest of Jarmila's children combined. When Johnny bought his first car, things got worse. It was a '57 Chevrolet convertible with a 265-cubic-inch, bored and stroked, high lift cam, dual quad carbs, and a three-speed on the floor. It was the era of the muscle cars, and Johnny had to have one. It only made sense: Johnny and Tommy had been listening to songs like The Hot Rod Lincoln long before either of them could drive.

Johnny's muscle car had to out-shine all the others. He bought as many chrome engine parts as he could, putting all his hard-earned money into his car. When he lifted the hood, the motor shined like a mirror. Johnny was in his glory days until one late evening, on the way home from seeing a movie in Cedar Rapids, his car broke down on Highway 151, near Walford. Nothing was open in the small town at that time of night, so Johnny left his car at the side of the road and hitchhiked home.

The next morning, Johnny and a mechanic returned to his car. When they opened the hood to make the repairs, there was nothing left to fix. Someone had stripped his beautiful chrome motor from the car. The theft ended Johnny's chrome era, but not the hot rodding.

Later, Tommy would say that Johnny not only lettered in sports, but he also lettered in speeding and drag racing. "Johnny was also a multi-vehicle letterman in falling asleep at the wheels of vehicles as several of the Amana bread trucks and one of his personal cars could attest to," Tommy said. "When he was not crashing a vehicle, he was picked up for speeding. Johnny was a real Dennis the Menace."

Jarmila tried to keep the boys out of trouble. She cooked a hot breakfast every morning before they headed off to school. Often, one of the neighbor boys arrived in Jarmila's kitchen in time to eat.

Meanwhile, John turned the small rural German bakery into a phenomenal success, servicing multiple states with German bakery products. In the 50s and 60s, the Amanas also became known for their shops making handmade products, their restaurants, and their agriculture.

Eva wrote home often. She and Frank continued to grow their family—this time with a daughter. Julie Ann Newman was born in Beb Herfedal,

Germany, on July 9, 1961. Two years later, on February 28, 1963, they had another boy—Steven Alan, who looked and acted so much like his intelligent father that everyone said he was "a chip off the old block." He quickly became known as "Chip" to family and friends. Now, the couple had three children under the age of four. Eva loved being a mother.

Later that year, Frank was reassigned to Fort Benning, in Columbus, Georgia, bringing them closer to John and Jarmila—something Eva had hoped to do. She wanted her children to know their grandparents, and this allowed them the opportunity to spend holidays together. Family had always been important to her; now that she had children of her own, it meant even more.

While Michael, Julie, and Chip were toddlers, Eva taught them to appreciate nature and the outdoors. She found ways for them to enjoy the Georgia sunshine year-round. Eva loved to be outside with them. Every day was an adventure. During summer months, the kids splashed in their own little swimming pool in the backyard. Sometimes, Eva took them to town to swim in the city pool or to enjoy the nearby Callaway Gardens. The Kool Aid flowed like water in the summer heat.

Of all the holidays, Christmas was Eva's favorite. She still remembered spending childhood Christmases in the Displaced Persons Camps, where the family hoped to receive gifts from strangers through the American Red Cross. Determined to create better memories for her children, she taught them the true meaning of Christmas and encouraged them to treasure their time together as a family.

Eva loved to bake. She and the children made cookies, and the scent of gingerbread filled their home and lifted their spirits. Their favorite was the old-fashioned Czech vanilla crescent Christmas cookie, the "vanilkové rohlíčky." They baked them every Christmas and there were never enough.

And the decorations! Eva bought a live fir Christmas tree and hung shimmering glass ornaments on every branch. On Christmas Eve, she prepared baked goose with potato dumplings. Eva always did more than most, to make up for the children's father being away at the holiday. They were happy and content.

For Eva, these years were golden. She had everything—her faith, her family, and her freedom. She was in love with life. And, because she remembered all that her parents left behind to escape Communism, she appreciated every moment. She had no way of anticipating what her future might hold. It was enough to be thankful for each day.

In 1965, several momentous events took place. Officials declared the Amana Colony a National Historic Landmark—a designation that would draw more tourists to the quaint seven-village colony already known for its restaurants and craft shops. For John and the bakery, this was good news.

That same year, Frank was transferred to Fort Rucker, in Ozark, Alabama. And, in June 1965, Eva's middle brother, Johnny, enlisted in the US Navy. He was 19 years old, and Eva was proud of his decision. The mischievous Dennis the Menace of the family had grown up. Jarmila shared the news with Eva.

"Johnny has joined the U.S. Navy," Jarmila said. "Your father and I drove him to the airport in Cedar Rapids. Tom will be lost without Johnny."

Jarmila knew Tommy would continue to work at the bakery after his brother joined the Navy. But she had underestimated Tom's ability to generate his own fun. The personable young boy quickly made friends with his classmates and formed a strong bond with a neighbor boy named Patrick. The two rode their bicycles everywhere together. It wasn't uncommon for them to pedal all the way to Marengo to swim in the city pool, taking the gravel roads nearly 15 miles each way.

Closer to home, Tom and Patrick liked to head for the railroad tracks a short distance from the bakery. The two pranksters filled balloons with water and carried them to the railroad overpass. When cars passed under the bridge on the country road, the boys dropped their balloons.

When Tom was 16, he and another friend, Russell, joined Patrick in a prank that amused some of their neighbors and offended others. After a few beers, the three boys climbed into their classmate's dilapidated 2-door Model

A Ford and went joyriding through the villages. The vehicle wasn't much to look at, with only the frame, four tires, a steering wheel, and a seat. There were no fenders and no roof, and the body was thin. The car had a swastika painted on the side and one boy brought two Nazi helmets, which the boys wore.

The teenagers took to the streets, driving through the quiet villages and saluting everyone in sight. Most laughed at the spectacle; the few that didn't approve, never complained. They understood the boys were out for fun and adventure and meant no harm.

After Johnny enlisted, the Navy assigned him to serve on the USS Van Voorhis (DE-1028), a destroyer escort based out of Newport, Rhode Island, that primarily conducted operations in the Western Atlantic.

The same month Johnny was aboard the ship, on June 16, 1965, the U.S. Army received Department of Defense authorization to organize the First Cavalry Division (Airmobile). Although the intensifying war in Vietnam provided the immediate impetus, the army had been contemplating such a division for several years—from at least 1960, when Frank trained to fly helicopters.

The First Cavalry had an increased troop mobility and included four times the number of aircraft in a standard army division. This would give the army the capability to move swiftly, an advantage countering the enemy's familiarity with the terrain, where the landscape and climate impeded American ground mobility.[xxxiii]

Eva and Frank were barely settled into their house at Fort Rucker, in Ozark, when the army reassigned him again. In August, as part of a massive troop buildup in the former French Indochina, Frank received orders for his first combat tour. He was on his way to Vietnam.

CHAPTER TWENTY-EIGHT

VIETNAM & THE SIXTIES

At the end of 1964, only about 23,300 U.S. troops, mostly advisors, were stationed in South Vietnam. By the close of 1965, that number had grown to 184,300, with the majority being Army soldiers.[xxxiv] During his tour in Vietnam, Frank sent a daily letter home to Eva. She saved them all. Among them was one written during the monsoon season. Frank's helicopter crashed, and he didn't think he would make it out alive. As he hid under the wreckage of the helicopter, surrounded by the Viet Cong, he found a scrap of paper and wrote on it:

"I am writing to you today to let you know that under all conditions and circumstances, I love you and our children."

Good fortune was with him that day. Frank was rescued and taken to safety. He wrote to Eva as he always did. With the letter, he enclosed the note he had written underneath the helicopter.

In July 1966, Frank completed his tour with the 14th Cavalry. He returned to the United States, where the Army assigned him to the 11th Air Assault Division, stationed at Fort Rucker in Alabama. Frank was a flight instructor and subsequently became Chief of the Foreign Military Training Division. Later, the 11th Air Assault Division became the 1st Cavalry Division, thus resurrecting one of the Army's most famed combat formations.

Frank came home from Vietnam, but the number of troops there continued to increase. It seemed the higher the number of troops grew, the lower public support for the war plummeted. On Aug 1,1966, Gallup Polls showed the American public support of the war had dropped from more than 52% to 37%, and the protest movement began.[xxxv]

Eva was 28 and sensed her young children were growing up too fast: Michael turned 6 that year; Julie, 4; and Chip, 3. Michael started school. Though her life revolved around her children, Eva was still a military wife. She helped Frank welcome foreign officers into the training school and often hosted them at their home. Together, they devoted themselves to the U.S. Army.

Eva and Frank led a disciplined military life in a world where society openly rebelled from following standard rules. Meanwhile, hemlines climbed upward: the younger generation wore skirts that ended at the upper thigh. The mini skirt was the fashion of choice.

In August 1966, Eva's brother, John Jr. was on the USS Van Voorhis when the ship rendezvoused with the destroyer escort USS Hammerberg guided missile frigate, the USS Leahy, and submarine USS Requin off Trinidad to participate in Operation Unitas VII through November. In 1966 and 1967, the warship made cruises around South America in which he visited several South American ports and took part in bilateral and multilateral exercises with warships of various South American countries.

John Jr. wrote to his brother about the hazing initiation the tadpoles received when they crossed the equator and the numerous ports they docked at. Johnny did not invent the term "drunken sailor," but he lived the tradition, eventually sporting rather large tattoos on each of his forearms.

Back in Iowa, John's bakery was attracting national attention. In September 1966, *Bakery Production and Marketing* magazine wrote a feature article about the Amana Bakery and the growth they had experienced under John Honolka's leadership. The article described how John's visionary approach turned the little bakery into a regional powerhouse.

Amana marries old fashioned hand work to work-saving equipment to get million dollar sales and practical efficiency.

Bread lovers in eight midwestern states are becoming acquainted with a brand name that once was known but in a very small section of central Iowa.

The name is Amana—now appearing on several dozen varieties of specialty breads and rolls distributed from Kansas City to the eastern counties of Illinois and Wisconsin, and from South Dakota to Missouri. Home base is the Amana Colonies, Amana, Iowa.

Expansion of the brand name and the product line traces back some 10 years. About 1955, a desire on the part of the Amana Bakery to expand the commercial opportunities was connected up with the talents of John Honolka, a baker recently arrived in the U.S. from the refugee camps of Europe. The marriage proved a happy one.

At that time, the Amana line of breads accounted for sales volume of approximately $9,000 per month. Sales figures are now running at better than $80,000 a month—and the prospects for a really major improvement are well in sight.

Up to this point, Amana has been largely a small town marketer. The only major markets exposed to the Amana brand have been Des Moines, Iowa and Omaha and Lincoln, Nebraska. But distribution (through local jobbers) is already arranged and citizens of both Kansas City and St. Louis, Mo., will be snacking on Amana label baked products this autumn. Chicago is definitely in Honolka's plans as well.

Wholesale bakers in the area have been quick to appreciate the immediate and continued acceptance given to Amana's line of variety breads. Several have taken on the line jobbing Amana's products on their own wholesale routes, enabling Amana to realize the distribution economics of "drop shipment" deliveries. This distribution factor, coupled with the fact that their one-pound varieties wholesale for 28¢ to 32¢, explains why this Iowa enterprise nets a profit on sales of 3 to 4 percent.

The Amana product is a large selection of variety breads and rolls. As many as 20 are offered at one time but Honolka is quick to add, "Customer preferences are always shifting. I watch sales carefully, and am always ready to drop a style and replace it with another as soon as demand drops." Honolka works with about a 25 percent casualty each year.

Honolka writes his own formulas—derived in part from his European background. His guide in selecting products is principally based on small 2-gallon market tests with employees and perhaps a restaurant or two located conveniently to the bakery. The aim, typical of variety breads, is to achieve a "home style" appearance.

The Amana Society Bakery is located in Upper South Amana in a distinctly rural setting. It is one among several that make up the Amana Colony. . .

Honolka has developed his own job descriptions. He established sanitation, for example, as a part of the job pattern of each worker. Each person is held responsible for keeping his respective work area and machinery clean and sanitary at all times and is expected to plan his work schedule accordingly.

Amana early user of poly bags

According to Honolka, an important contributor to Amana's sales growth has been the wrapper. Glassine and paper wrappers were replaced by poly bags. And the labels have been redesigned and up-graded with the assistance of a packaging supplier. The Amana logo-type, a wagon wheel, long a hallmark of the Amana design, has been retained. However, it has been embellished with three and four-color printing. Overall, the label tells the type of product, the price, information on ingredient contents, etc.—all in bright combinations of eye-appealing colors.

In Honolka's view, the poly bags have yielded several easy to identify benefits. These include outstanding visibility, an impression of cleanliness, and product protection. On this final point, Honolka feels the poly bag adds "days" to product freshness—a particularly important feature in the light of the extensive truck routes maintained.

Why buy Amana "home style" breads? In Honolka's view, "Certainly, there is no question of the appeal of a quality variety bread." It's an appeal that seems principally to folks who have known home-made breads in their past. People with rural backgrounds or from recent European family stock are the most typical. This usually means the purchaser is older…perhaps 40-45. The exceptions are young people who have traveled outside the United States and who have discovered the pleasure of the variety of breads. "I'm confident," he concludes, "this share of the bread market can grow."

Jarmila was pleased that John's hard work had been recognized in the national trade publication of the baking industry. John accepted the praise but continued to focus on growing the business. He wasn't finished yet.

Meanwhile, sentiments toward the Vietnam War continued to shift. On March 25, 1967, over 5,000 protestors marched in Chicago, Illinois to protest the war. They cheered when civil rights leader Martin Luther King, Jr. declared the Vietnam War "a blasphemy against all that America stands for."[xxxvi]

Later that spring, in May 1967, Johnny was honorably discharged from the Navy. He was 21 and spent two more years in the Naval Reserves. John Jr. returned to the Amana Colonies and bought another muscle car: a blue 1969 Chevelle super sport, 396 cubic inch, 4 speed. Once again, he demonstrated his ability to fall asleep at the wheel and destroy cars. His younger brother Tommy declared, "Every time Johnny crawled into a car, I could imagine God sending an angel and saying, "Anchors aweigh boys, here he comes!"

Johnny worked for his father's prosperous bakery operation. By the time he was 22, he had helped to build a distribution network to sell the Amana Bakery products throughout Texas, Louisiana and Mississippi—driving up to 18 hours in a non-air-conditioned bread truck to deliver the orders in the hot southern states. In June 1968, he drove to Texas to deliver bread in the Dallas/Fort Worth area. There, he pulled into Powell's Hamburgers— an "American Graffiti" style hamburger stand on Park Row in Arlington, Texas—where he claimed the phone number of the prettiest girl there. Her name was Sandra. He called her. He dated her. And on September 6, 1969, he married her. The couple had a daughter and a son.

There were changes taking place in Eva and Frank's home during the late sixties, too. The family had just adopted their first cat, a Siamese named Sam. Julie, a cat-lover like her mom, rejoiced. Then, new orders arrived. In March 1967, Frank, still an Artillery Officer, was assigned to the Advanced Artillery School at Fort Sill, Oklahoma. The family moved to Oklahoma, bringing Sam along.

Frank excelled in the academic setting—many officers and instructors commented on his scholarship and leadership. Soon he was assigned to the Foreign Military Training Division, where Eva helped him with his work. The two both understood the problems of newcomers entering a strange land. When Eva invited foreign students to their home for dinner, she took time to learn their backgrounds and religion and planned her meals accordingly. She knew that dumplings, sauerkraut and pork roast were the Czech equivalent of potatoes, salad and steak in the US.

After 21 months in Oklahoma, the Army wanted Frank back in Ozark, Alabama. It was nearly Christmas, so the family opened their gifts early, then traveled to their new home on Christmas Day, 1968. This time, Frank and Eva bought their first home. It was on a large corner lot with a creek at the back of their property, and they intended to retire there. Mike and Chip were thrilled with the move, but Julie pouted. She hated moving almost as much as she disliked having her father away all the time.

Just three months after their return to Alabama, in March 1969, Frank was reassigned again; he was headed to Vietnam, to serve as Commanding Officer, 131st Aviation Company, 212th Combat Aviation Battalion, 1st Aviation Brigade. He would be away for an entire year, flying missions into the jungles of Vietnam.

Eva did her best to keep the children entertained while Frank was gone. They had a fish tank in the living room, and cages with frogs, crabs, and lizards. Several times, they drove 1 ½ hours away, to Panama Beach, Florida, for the day. It was a good life, but the children still missed their father. And, always, Eva feared for Frank's safety.

CHAPTER TWENTY-NINE

A DECADE OF MOURNING

Eva rushed around the house in February 1970, preparing for Frank's return in five short days. She hung new shower curtains, fussed with the bedspread, and planned a menu of his favorite foods to cook on his arrival. The kids were excited to see their father again. He had been away from home for nearly a year. Michael, 11, Julie, 8, and Steven, 7, could not wait for him to walk through the door.

Tuesday morning, February 24th, at 6:45 a.m., Eva heard a car pull into her driveway. She glanced out the window and saw three officers striding up the sidewalk in their dress uniforms.

Eva usually welcomed soldiers from the nearby military base, but she had not expected this visit. A sense of dread settled over her. She knew something was terribly wrong. When they knocked, she opened the door. The officers stood ramrod straight: a military chaplain and two officers from Fort Ruckers.

Eva strained to hear their words through the loud roar that filled her head. "Mrs. Eva Newman?"

She nodded. Her body had suddenly gone numb; she was unable to speak.

"Ma'am. The Commanding General of the United States Army has entrusted me to express his deep regret that your husband, Lt. Col. Frank Charles Newman, was killed in the line of duty, on February 23, 1970. . ."

A low moan escaped Eva's lips. Her legs buckled.

Frank died when his Army Mohawk reconnaissance aircraft malfunctioned. He ejected, but his parachute failed to open. The plane crashed at Phu Bai, Vietnam on Feb. 23, 1970, five days before he was scheduled to complete his second tour in Vietnam. He was 42. His death ripped Eva and her children apart. They had purchased their home in Ozark, Alabama, where he and Eva planned to live with their three children. Instead, they buried him in the cemetery there.

Eva was 32. Her faith carried her through a time of shock and mourning. Later, she told the story. "I became a widow with three little children, two boys and a girl," she said. "When the time came, I pinned Frank's wings on my son's chest. I was proud to be the wife of a soldier who gave his all." Although she didn't know it at the time, Frank's death started a decade of tribulations for Eva to overcome.

Major General Delk M. Oden, Commanding General at Ft. Rucker, and Commandant of the Army Aviation School, presented LTC Frank C. Newman with posthumous awards at a ceremony in his office. Eva and her children were there to accept the awards.

Major General Oden remarked that LTC Newman had enlisted in the U.S. Army in Germany in 1952 and was stationed at Ft. Rucker as Chief of the Foreign Military Training Division from 1966 to 1968.

"LTC Newman, a native of Czechoslovakia, was a man who appreciated life in this country for his wife and his family," Oden said.

The citation accompanying the Legion of Merit—the nation's second-highest award for outstanding achievement—noted:

Frank Newman "consistently demonstrated efficient responsiveness to the myriad problems inherent in conducting operations in a hostile combat environment.

"Through the application of dynamic leadership, rare foresight, and sound principles of management, he was able to direct his company in attaining an exemplary record of mission accomplishments.

"Through his courage, initiative and fidelity, LTC Newman earned the respect and admiration of all with whom he served and made a material contribution in the free world effort to thwart Communist aggression in the Republic of Vietnam."

In an emotional tribute to her husband, Eva spoke about Frank Newman later that summer.

During my life, I have spent much time on the speaking and lecture circuit. In this 'Magnificent Obsession,' I am motivated not only by Frank Charles Newman's life and service to our nation, but by my own desire to pay back, at least a little, to the nation which adopted us.

I am keenly aware that the Lord has a mission for my life, and that—in a manner of speaking—it is a continuation of Frank's mission to serve his God, Honor, Duty, and Country. While Frank's mortal duty on this earth is done, the mission nevertheless continues, until the point I am silenced.

LTC Frank Charles Newman's service to his adopted land, and to the land to which he gave so much, lasted some eighteen years. In this timeframe, and as a member of the United States Army, Frank rose from Private to the Grade of Lieutenant Colonel.

LTC Newman was not simply an aviator, he was a passionate aviator. He amassed some 3,500 flying hours and was proficient in 22 types of both fixed-wing and rotary aircraft. At the time of his death, LTC Newman held status as a "Master Aviator."

In many ways an unlikely soldier, Frank held numerous awards and decorations, which include the Distinguished Flying Cross, The Legion of Merit, the Bronze Star, Vietnamese Order of the Palm, 22 Air Medals and numerous additional awards and commendations.

Frank Charles Newman has left a priceless legacy. He was a man of true humility, as most heroes are. He was a man of gentleness. He was sensitive, kind, and caring—an ideal husband and father.

In addition to these attributes, Frank was a man of unbending integrity and uncompromising principles and ethics. He did not find it necessary to speak or lecture on these qualities: he lived them. He was, to many, the ideal commanding officer. He asked nothing of others that he had not done or was not willing to do. He was honored and respected by his soldiers.

As the firing party rendered its final salute, one envisions the riderless horse, boots reversed in the stirrups, saber slung from the saddle, led by the solemn soldier. The Warrior is borne to his final resting place, flag-draped coffin on the artillery caisson. This vision is somewhat metaphorical except for the firing party, the sounding of "Taps," and the "Missing Man Formation" flown by Frank Newman's fellow aviators from nearby Fort Rucker, Alabama.

LTC Frank Charles Newman now rests not far from nearby Fort Rucker, a post made better for his having been there; an Army made better for his having proudly served in it.

Death came to LTC Frank Charles Newman out of the soft blue of a Vietnamese sky. It was his time, and those of us who honor his life, his service, his legacy, will always be tempted to ask "Why?"

I will not attempt to answer that question, for to do so lies far beyond my power. Suffice it to say that Frank Charles Newman, LTC of Artillery, U.S. Army, is one more immortal like in the "Long Blue Line" which dates to the very founding of the Republic. The Army is better for Frank simply having served in it. We are better people, for simply having known Frank, for having loved him, having experienced his love, for having served alongside and with him. Most of all, for being inspired by his example of "God, Honor, Duty and Country."

Eva reflected on the accomplishments of her husband. The man she had been reluctant to marry had become the love of her life: LTC Frank Charles Newman. Born Frantisek Neuman in Nepomuk, Czechoslovakia, Frank himself had fled Czechoslovakia and was a refugee of Communism, later changing his name to Frank Newman.

The young man had been a college preparatory student in Prague during the war. In 1946, he was accepted as a law student at Charles University, the oldest university in Central Europe, as a law student. But while he was a law student, Frank became interested in politics and joined with other students in protesting the new Czechoslovakian government that was controlled by the Soviet Communists. He fled the secret police in 1948 but was captured in 1949. Frank was a leader among the prisoners. He escaped to Vienna, then to French occupied Germany, ending up in the Bad Wurzbach displaced person's camp. While there in 1952, he enlisted in the United States Army under the Lodge Act of 1952 and later emigrated to the United States, where he underwent training to become an officer. He worked himself through the ranks from a private (E1) to become a highly decorated master aviator and commissioned officer "mustang" of the 101st aviation company.

In 1971, Eva still reeled from her loss. It had been more than a year since Frank's death, and she sought stability for her children. She remarried, but the marriage was a difficult one, plagued by tragedies and abuse.

The couple's first baby, John Zeke, was born November 10, 1971. He died three days later.

Three years later, they tried again. Eva gave birth to a beautiful baby boy, Sidney, on March 3, 1974. The little boy was only a toddler when he drowned in a tragic accident, at the age of three, on July 8, 1977.

Somehow, Eva's faith survived. Her marriage didn't. The couple divorced in 1978.

During the years when Eva struggled to create a new life for herself and her children, the world also changed for her parents and her brother, Johnny. Her father retired from the bakery in 1975, at 66. He and Jarmila would spend the next years of their life together, enjoying their grandchildren. John had set aside his dreams of the bakery he had hoped to own and expand into national prominence—an accomplishment the family believed would have happened, if only he had owned the bakery or had the support of those who did.

As John Sr. retired, Johnny also left the Amana Bakery behind. He turned his automobile obsession into a career, working in sales and as a sales manager at various dealerships in Texas, where he would work for over 40 years. He became known as "JJ" because no one could remember or pronounce "Honolka." Johnny and Sandy remained married 51 years, until his death on November 22, 2020.

Two years after Eva's ill-fated second marriage, on a day that had always been precious to her, Eva experienced yet another tragedy. It was June 14, 1980—Flag Day across America—and Eva's older son, Michael's 21st birthday. They planned to celebrate with a cake that evening. The day was hot and sunny. Seventeen-year-old Chip headed out that morning to meet friends at the beach, but he rushed back into the house minutes later.

"Mom, I forgot to hang the flag today!"

He raised the Stars and Stripes on their flagpole and raced out the door, again, on his way to Panama Beach, Florida, for a swim in the ocean.

Later that afternoon, Chip slept in the back seat of the car as his friend drove toward home. Chip never knew he was in a car accident. The impact tossed Chip from the vehicle. He never woke up. His friend sustained minor injuries.

Eva prayed on her knees so long that day that she could not walk when she finally stood up again. The American flag that draped Lt. Col. Frank Newman's casket ten years earlier covered the casket of Steve Allen "Chip" Newman, Eva's third son, at his funeral.

Eva stayed strong for her remaining children, Julie and Mike. Later, she spoke about that day with gratitude. "As devastated as I was by Chip's death, I was still proud to be an American," she said. "I was grateful for the freedom to practice my faith, the privilege to pray, and the ability to take my son's casket into a church for his funeral. All of these are freedoms taken for granted by many Americans, but unavailable in some countries."

Still, whenever she spoke of Chip, Eva fought to swallow a lump in her throat. Her face was shadowed in sadness. And when she saw Chip's trumpet, Eva's eyes filled with tears.

On July 4, 1980, just a few weeks after Chip's death, Eva received a letter from her father. John wrote with advice on the upkeep of her property and her income. He concluded the letter with a request.

"Just to let you know, in case something should happen to me, this is my wish: to be buried next to Frank and Big Shot (John's pet name for his grandson, Chip.) I do not want any expensive funeral, just a simple one without a church service or organist, without a vault and the cheapest coffin.

"Because I have no one here I can talk to, I have to rely on you to see to it that it's done. I lived a simple life, and I want to fade away simply."

Though he and Jarmila lived in Arlington, Texas, at that time, John always had a close relationship with his grandson Chip. Clearly, he wanted Eva to handle his final wishes when the time came to lay him to rest.

CHAPTER THIRTY

NEW BEGINNINGS

Frank and Chip's deaths reduced Eva's income. Military pay for widows was small, and the Social Security income Chip had received from his father ceased at his own death. Eva looked for a job.

When a friend told her about an open position with the State of Alabama, Eva applied. The job was as a tour guide at the First White House of the Confederacy, in Montgomery, Alabama. It was 90-miles, one-way, from where she lived in Ozark, and it required a deep knowledge of the history of Alabama. Determined to win the position, Eva studied diligently to pass the test; and she did.

For the first year, she drove the distance from Ozark to Montgomery every day. She never complained, and quickly became known for her hospitality and grace. After a year, Eva sold the home she and Frank had chosen, moving closer to her job. Because she was generous with others, people thought she had money. In truth, Eva barely made enough to make ends meet. She learned to live frugally, so she could continue to pay her own way and still have a little left to share when needed.

Eva's father died on April 26, 1983, in Arlington, Texas. At 73, he looked older than his years. Though the struggles of life had etched his face, his warm expression, shining eyes and sense of humor remained to the end. It was difficult to believe that John Honolka, the accomplished athlete and businessman who survived the Nazis, Russian Communism, prisons and refugee camps, was gone.

Eva honored his written request for a simple service. She gave the eulogy at his funeral on April 28, 1983, at the Moore Funeral Home Chapel in Arlington, Texas.

"Jesus taught us that the truth about each man lay in his spirit and not the physical world. Religions and temples are built by man, but God's temple is man, and wherever we are, we are always in a place of worship. Life is the medium through which we seek to work out that purpose. When that purpose is fulfilled, it is time for us to return home once again.

"We are here today to say farewell to our beloved father, grandfather, and husband. We come with respect and admiration, with gratitude in our hearts for his courageous leadership—for he was a pioneer in a difficult time and a difficult era—but nevertheless a pioneer to this great land called America.

"He was a man of great physical strength, participating in competitive sports. He skied, loved hockey and soccer. Dad reveled in challenge, and he challenged life.

"John had great mental strength and abilities that made him take the promise of opportunity that this country offered and became successful in business. John worked hard and long hours, because work gave him dignity and he was a dignified man.

"He loved this earth and all its natural beauty—and he took from this earth only what he needed—he never wasted. Dad was in quest of knowledge, to know the earth upon which he lived, and he expressed that love in the things he planted in his garden and the joy he expressed when he was surrounded by nature.

"He was a giant in the community of businessmen. He marketed bread in several states, from Iowa to Louisiana. His innovative approach took the loaves out of waxed paper and put them in the now familiar poly bags for greater convenience, freshness, and product visibility.

"John Honolka was not too lazy to bend over; he worked from 5 a.m. to 10 p.m. in his pursuit of happiness with hope, to become a successful businessman.

"He was a man—he had his faults—but he was humble and always responsible.

"He was a good man, and his goodness manifested itself in the love he had for his grandchildren, the little people in his Honolka clan. To them, I am sure he would have said this: 'It is necessary to feel a sense of history.'

"You are part of what has come before, and part of what is yet to come. Being *this surrounded, you are not alone. Do not frivolously use the time that is yours to spend. Cherish it—that each day may bring new growth, not selfish, but rather in service. What may be in the future tide of time, never allow a day to pass that did not add to what was understood before.*

"John Honolka has gone home. His spirit lay down his body because it was finished with the work on this earth, and John moves into the great expansion where he is part of the great universe. He is now with God in the endless time of eternity. As each of us—his five children—part of him continues, and it does make a difference that John Honolka lived. The world is a better place because he was in it.

"For liberty, he sacrificed a lot. But the divine gift of liberty is God's recognition of man's greatness and man's dignity. So, liberty is in the sweetness of life and the power of growth.

"Under the spell of heavenly memorials, John never ceased to dream of liberty and aspire to its possession, until it was caught up in his embrace, in a great and abiding nation.

"I will miss my dad. I feel the pain and loneliness, and life seems bleak and cold. But this is life, can you see? That dust to dust returned, but Godly souls and sweet memories shall ever remain—I shall rise again."

They buried John next to Frank and "Big Shot" in Westview Cemetery, Ozark, Alabama. Jarmila continued to live in Texas.

Through her work at the First White House of the Confederacy, Eva found a new purpose for her life.

"When Frank died, I absolutely had to influence the young people about patriotism and the honor of it in our flag, and what it means to us as a nation," Eva said. She believed her position at the First White House of the Confederacy provided that opportunity. It was a position she would hold for thirty-three years. She loved her home in Montgomery, where she had huge banana trees and monstrous elephant ear plants. It was the only place in her life where she put down roots. For her, Montgomery was "home."

Eva was a gracious host. She loved gardening, nature walks, reading, and singing. She played the piano, the harmonica and the accordion. She could sew and was an excellent cook. She decorated cakes and baked many for special occasions at the First White House of the Confederacy. One day, Eva was surprised to see a Czech Republic Officer walk into the building where she worked. The officer was attending Air University at Maxwell Air Base.

"I never believed that day would come that I would have Czech Republic officers walk in. Frank never got to finish what he started, so I had to sponsor and teach these Czechs," she said.

Henry Howard, also a tour guide for the First White House of the Confederacy, said Eva's tours always generated an emotional response from visitors. "She earned the right to become an American. When you think of someone who is from a different country and is more patriotic than you, it really stirs you up inside."

Eva Newman's love and pride for her country showed through to the people she met and reminded others what it was to be a good American. She befriended another staff member—Sergeant Philip Carroll "PC" Callahan, whom Governor Wallace had appointed to the Alabama White House police force. Often, PC surveyed the White House, where Eva supervised the receptionists. They spent hours talking about history and democracy. PC was like a younger brother looking out for his big sister. Each of them loved life and had a great sense of humor.

PC had also met Jarmila on several occasions when she visited her daughter. The two had engaged in deep conversations about history and world affairs. They shared many of the same interests. PC admired all that John and Jarmila had done to bring their family to America. In 1986, the year before PC's scheduled to retirement from the State Capitol, Eva's mother fell ill in Arlington, Texas. Unable to leave her job to be with her mother, Eva fretted about how to best care for Jarmila. Without hesitation, PC Callahan resigned from his position and moved to Texas to care for Jarmila, spending his days conversing with her and offering the companionship she needed. It was a sacrifice Eva never forgot.

Jarmila had always longed to return to her homeland but two years and three months before the Czech Republic won its freedom from Communism and reopened the borders, her health worsened. After suffering from chest pains for several days, Jarmila saw her doctor, who recommended a cardiologist who could not see her until the following day. He scheduled her for tests next morning.

The appointment was too late. Jarmila died of a massive heart attack that night.

After her funeral, they found Jarmila's packed luggage under her bed. It contained clothes for one last trip to her beloved homeland in the Czech Republic. Jarmila never forgot her heritage or gave up her citizenship. She never knew she had dual citizenship. She was an American but died a Czech at heart. Her most loving memories were there, in her homeland.

***

After Jarmila's death in 1987, PC Callahan returned to Montgomery, where his superiors reinstated his full benefits until his retirement. He remained a friend until he died on May 11, 2017.

Eva was 50 years old when her mother died. She had always vowed to "appreciate life as it is given to us by a power beyond ourselves." She faced her mother's death the same way she had handled the other challenges of her life, leaning on her faith to sustain her.

All five of John and Jarmila's adult children gathered for Jarmila's funeral in 1987. From left: Don, Eva, Vlasta (Patricia), Tom, and John. Jarmila made the dress Vlasta is wearing.

CHAPTER THIRTY-ONE

SPEAKING OUT FOR FREEDOM

Eva saw her patriotism as both an honor and an obligation. "We gave everything—our heritage, and our language, for an intangible called freedom. It is my utmost obligation to give until my last breath to a nation that so graciously adopted us," she said.

In July 1989, only a few months before Eva's beloved Czechoslovakia would finally regain its freedom from Communism, a reporter for *The Alabama Journal* interviewed Eva in Montgomery. The newspaper published a lengthy article that focused on Eva's lifetime commitment to the cause of freedom and praised her for speaking out to civic clubs and organizations to promote the flag. The story included details not shared in previous articles.

Born in Trutnov, Czechoslovakia in 1937, Mrs. Newman came into the world about the same time the German troops moved into the mountains of her native country. By the time she was in elementary school, German planes were bombing the cities.

"I started to school in 1943," she said. "I remember the bombings and the food lines and the terror of occupation by another nation over you."

"I could hear the bombs dropping, and I remember the schoolhouse shaking. You were rushed down into the school basement. When the bombs stopped and you came up from the basement, you did not know if your house was still standing."

"You don't forget something like that. I think fear is something we seldom forget."

Eva talked about her memories of the prison where she and her sister and brothers saw children die of malnutrition.

"When babies died, the guards would come and pick up their little bodies. They would put them in a paper sack and take them away. It was a nightmare. My little brother, Johnny, was 18 months old and had malnutrition. The peppers they were feeding us were eating his stomach up. The surroundings were filthy and lacked toilet facilities.

"I remember we were sitting there on the straw, and my mother was picking fleas and ticks out of my little brother's hair," she said.

Her story served as an inspiration to readers. Everyone admired the gracious woman who had lived her life in search of freedom. The Velvet Revolution happened that same year. It was a non-violent transition of power in what was then Czechoslovakia, occurring from November 17-28, 1989. Students and older citizens staged popular demonstrations against the one-party government of the Communist Party of Czechoslovakia. The result was the end of 41 years of one-party rule in Czechoslovakia. In June 1990, Czechoslovakia held its first democratic elections since 1946. (Later, on December 31, 1992, Czechoslovakia peacefully split into two countries: the Czech Republic and the Slovak Republic.)[xxxvii]

Eva was a frequent guest at a variety of meetings and organizations, where she captivated audiences with her personal story. From 1989 through the next two decades, she dedicated her time to speaking out for freedom. As Eva toured the state for speaking appearances, the press took notice. Soon, the small woman with the Czech accent was in big demand. Reporters wanted to know more about her life and found new ways to tell her story.

One such article appeared in *The Montgomery Weekly Advertiser* on October 19, 1991. A staff writer asked Eva a casual question about the fruit trees in her yard and ended up writing a full story titled: "1991 Asian Fruit Tree A Living Legacy from Dad."

Eva Honolka Newman is 'bananas' about elephant ears and banana plants. She has dozens of them lining her yard. But, to her, the 25-feet tall banana trees and elephant ears as big as car hoods are more than a hobby. They are a living memorial to the husband she lost in Vietnam.

Ms. Newman's husband, LTC Frank Charles Newman, left their three children and their home in Ozark, AL, to be an army pilot during the Vietnam War.

"My boys were always asking me, "What's it like where Daddy is?" she said. "I'd tell them 'It's a jungle with lots of green.'"

But Ms. Newman wanted to give her children a better idea of what the jungle was like, so she encouraged her husband to smuggle a banana plant bulb from Vietnam.

When her husband was given leave, Ms. Newman met him in Hawaii and got the "illegally" imported Vietnam banana plant. And, while in Hawaii, she also brought back an elephant ear plant. Once back in Ozark, Ms. Newman put the fist-sized banana bulb in a pot in her home.

That March, Mr. Newman was expected to return home from the war. Five days before his return, he was killed in action. That spring, Eva decided to plant the last gift from her husband.

"One day, I looked out there and saw these two leaves growing out, and lo and behold…" she said. Her plants had begun to grow and grow until fall, when the banana tree soared to more than 30 feet and was so wide her arms could not reach around it.

Everyone in the small town of Ozark, AL, knew about Ms. Newman. "They'd say: 'Eva's gone bananas with those banana plants.'"

She even "slipped a banana leaf into the church" one day when the townspeople were showing off their large fruit and vegetables. "Everyone said, 'What's that?' And I said, "It's my harvest."

Aside from the interest it created in other people, the towering plants, nested next to the gigantic elephant ears, were ideal for the children, who were then able to get a taste of the jungle and their father.

"My children have not stopped looking for that missing link—their father," she said. "The plant is sort of like a living memorial, if you know what I mean."

Every fall, the towering stalks of the banana tree are cut down to about 1 to 2 feet and hauled away. The stump is then fertilized as it waits through the spring until summer when temperatures rise to the 80's or 90's. The plant spurts over the roof in the six months of tropical-like weather.

Since then, Ms. Newman has moved to Montgomery and planted her banana plants and elephant ears in her yard. Over the years, Eva gave more than 65 banana plants to friends and relatives in Alabama, Georgia, Texas and Kansas, and she never charges a cent.

"I would no more sell them than the man on the moon," she said. "They were given to me to pass along."

Eva's banana trees.

Vlasta with an elephant ear plant.

Many years later, during February 2020, Eva's brother Don and his wife Sharon traveled to Ozark, AL. They stopped by Eva's former residence, where the banana trees and elephant ears had clearly survived, 50 years and counting.

By 1992, Eva had expanded her speaking appearances once again. Her children were adults, with jobs of their own, and she still felt called to serve as the voice of freedom. That year, the *Montgomery Weekly Advertiser* found another opportunity to interview Eva, with the resulting story, "I Feel Like the Lord Gave Me A Mission."

Let it be said Eva Newman loves God, country, and people in general. A state employee and Capitol receptionist, Mrs. Newman likens herself and the five others to salesmen, whether on duty at the State Capitol or at the First White House of the Confederacy.

"We are like salesmen who are selling the State of Alabama to the public," she said, adding, "We believe in our product."

Although Mrs. Newman spends a lot of time conducting tours and giving directions, her duties do not end there.

"On one hand," she said, "we have information, and on the other hand is the relational element. Both of those must come together to make an impact on people," she said. "People respond best when we relate information that is meaningful. It's our job as receptionists and guides to make it easy on our listeners," she said.

"How do you know what people want?" Mrs. Newman asked rhetorically. "The answer is simple," she said. "It has nothing to do with the subject or how articulate we are. It has everything to do with people."

Mrs. Newman philosophized that every person wants attention and that she, as a receptionist, demonstrates that she is paying attention to her public by recognizing them and what is important to them.

"I know of no better way to relate to the public than by bringing them a caring attitude, " Mrs. Newman said. "An attitude shows in our posture, facial expression, tone of voice. In all of these we communicate to our listeners, 'I recognize your presence and your importance.'"

Mrs. Newman's philosophy is illustrated in an incident that occurred one day during a tour for senior citizens. The bus driver had a heart attack, Mrs. Newman said. After they called paramedics, they were faced with keeping down the anxiety level of a large group of people. "We shared cookies, coffee and tea with them," she recalled. "It's important to have compassion for their situation."

She said the group was there for three or four hours before they were picked up by another bus.

"The job drains you, but it's rewarding, because you are selling your state." Mrs. Newman said.

She said because you need to be physically fit to do what she does, she works out at a local gymnasium. She also gets somewhat of a workout while conducting tours of the Capitol. She routinely avoids the elevator and walks the three flights of stairs at the Capitol because visitors frequently take the stairs. . .

She is a military widow and had six children. She has out-lived four of her five sons. Her two remaining children are Michael David, 33, an electrical engineer in Marietta, GA, and Julie Ann, 31, who is in Human Resources in Birmingham. . .

Mrs. Newman also does personal testimonials to high schools, civic groups and the boy scouts.

"She visited my Kiwanis Club and held the group spellbound throughout the period she talked, mostly about her own life's tragedies and triumphs," said Frank Mastin, Jr., The Montgomery Weekly Advertiser Editor and Publisher. Mr. Mastin is a member of the Good Morning Kiwanis Club in Montgomery.

A State Employee for 10 years, Mrs. Newman never took a vacation. Instead, she has devoted all her time to her job and speaking engagements. "I feel like the Lord gave me a mission, and that is to go and tell my story."

Eva continued her presentations, traveling to any location where she was invited to talk about freedom. The inspiring woman mesmerized everyone who heard her story. After listening to one of her speeches, John Rosenblatt, a visiting associate professor at Auburn University, summarized the response of the crowd.

"Your story moved each one of us, and your pride in being an American citizen came out loud and clear. I think you should make an appearance in each high school in the entire state of Alabama, and wherever else that is possible. Many members of the Armed Forces could improve their fighting spirit after being motivated by your most outstanding presentation," Rosenblatt said. "Old King Solomon would have approved of Mrs. Newman, in his infinite wisdom," he concluded. "Who can find a virtuous woman? For her price is far above rubies."

In January 1993, Czechoslovakia completed what historians refer to as the "velvet divorce," resulting in the country's separation into two new entities: the Czech Republic and Slovakia. It was another milestone in the transition of Eva's homeland. Though she was happy to see her country return to independence, she now viewed freedom as a precious commodity to be protected with vigilance.

That year, Eva traveled over 3,000 miles and spoke 60 times, all in her free time, and at her own expense, always dressed in red, white and blue. She continued to serve as supervisor of the Capital Receptionists with the State of Alabama in Montgomery, and to sponsor International Officer Students, primarily for the Czech and Slovak Republics who visited Maxwell AFB.

Eva described her motivation as a divine calling to go and tell that Jesus Christ is Lord, and to talk about freedom. "It's not easy," she said, "because I have feelings. But if I ever get to the point of not feeling, I will quit."

"It is my way of paying back the nation that so graciously adopted us," Eva said. "Those of us who have lived without freedom, liberty, and justice, will always treasure them dearly in our hearts and souls."

On June 9, 1993, just before Flag Day, Eva captivated yet another reporter with her insistence that Americans should celebrate Flag Day, as ardently as they do the Fourth of July. This time, it was Kareem Crayton, with the *East Montgomery Weekly.*

"Everyone celebrates the 4th of July, but how many people celebrate Flag Day?" asked a stately Eva Newman. "And, just as every American has a special reason to observe the occasion, so does she."

Crayton wrote of Eva's endurance of the Nazi occupation during WWII, the Communist takeover that followed, and her family's long, dangerous journey as refugees and immigrants. He told of husband's service to America, and his death in Vietnam. He wrote that, of Eva's three surviving children, one son was born on Flag Day, and another died on Flag Day.

Eva Honolka Newman often spoke to groups about the importance of honoring the American flag.

The reporter included the fact that the last chore completed by Eva's son, Chip, was to hang the American Flag in celebration of Flag Day, as he always did. He noted the pain Eva endured when she lost Chip, killed by a drunk driver later that day.

Despite the sadness connected with the day, Mrs. Newman has maintained her regard for Flag Day.

"My pride for the stars and stripes just goes deeper and deeper," she said.

Lecturing at local schools and civic organizations, Mrs. Newman has committed herself to spreading ideas about patriotism. "Americans just don't have as much pride in their country as they used to," she said. "Patriotism is the very heart and soul of an individual and a country…"

In Mrs. Newman's hands was the same flag the military gave her at her husband's funeral. "What we are celebrating is more than just the flag," Mrs. Newman said, clutching the tightly folded cloth of white stars and red stripes. "It is the symbol of what we are as individuals and as a country."

Although she admits that her story is an American dream, Mrs. Newman politely shies away from taking credit for the accomplishment. "What I have done is what everyone can do. That is the beauty of the United States," she said.

CHAPTER THIRTY-TWO

EVA'S LIFE'S WORK IS RECOGNIZED

Eva had been sharing her story since she was a young girl of 17. Now, she was 56, and her commitment to advocate for freedom had never wavered. Her entire life, she had preached freedom. "We arrived there hungry, torn, scarred, and scared, but there was the promise of opportunity to follow happiness with hope," she declared.

It was inevitable that Eva's passionate presentations would draw the notice of patriots in her hometown. But her words had reverberated far beyond the boundaries of her state. She was surprised to learn she had attracted the attention of The National Society for Daughters of the American Revolution (DAR)—a women's organization founded in 1890 and composed of descendants of Americans freedom fighters.

A non-profit group, the DAR proudly celebrates women who are directly descended from a person involved in the United States' struggle for independence. Boasting of more than one million members in their 125-year history, they promote education and patriotism and present awards to American citizens for outstanding contributions to the nation. The prestigious Medal of Honor goes to native-born American citizens and the Americanism Medal to naturalized citizens.

On Tuesday, March 8, 1994, the National Society, Daughters of the American Revolution, bestowed the Americanism Medal to Eva Honolka Newman, of Montgomery, Alabama. At the time they presented the medal to Eva, the DAR had only awarded eight medals to "outstanding naturalized American citizens" in its first 104 years.

Eva dedicated much of her life carrying the torch for freedom. Here she speaks in front of the American flag she championed.

Just one month later, she was also recognized by the community of Montgomery, AL, where she had spent so many years serving as an ambassador for her state. During their 20th Annual Volunteer of the Year Event on April 22, 1994, Eva's hometown newspaper, *The Montgomery Weekly Advertiser*, selected her for their highest honor: The Sustained Superior Performance Award. In announcing their choice, the publication declared:

"The naturalized American citizen has launched her own crusade to sell America, traveling the country telling her story of escape from her native Czechoslovakia and lauding the country that adopted her and her family. Her volunteer efforts include sponsorship of international officers stationed at Maxwell AirForce Base, Girls State, Boys State and the Hugh O'Brien Foundation.

That August, Eva and her sister Patricia traveled together to the country they had fled 44 years earlier. Their hearts raced as they stepped off the plane and breathed the air of their homeland. For the first time in over four decades, they stood on Czech Republic soil—formerly known as Czechoslovakia.

Eva was eleven when she and her family fled her Communist-controlled country for freedom. They believed Communism wouldn't last longer than four years, and they expected to return to their homeland, then. Over time, as the Soviet regime continued their tyranny over the Czechoslovakian people, the Honolkas came to understand they might never go home again. Yet, here she and Patricia stood. Their journey home had taken ten times longer than her father predicted. During their two-week visit, they were stunned to see many familiar places of their childhood were still intact.

"Nothing had really changed that much in all these years," said Eva. "The house where I was born, in Trutnov in 1937, is still there, and people are still living in it. My father's factory stood just like it did when we escaped. It was confiscated by the government without any compensation and was never returned to my family. It is now being used as a beauty shop, school kitchen, and for apartments."

Their visit was bittersweet. Together, they searched for documentation to support the family's existence, but someone had erased all records. "It was as though we were never there," Patricia said. "We found a record of my birth certificate, but nothing else. No deeds to verify land or building ownership. No marriage certificate from my parents' wedding. Nothing."

One Thursday in the fall of 1994, Eva spoke to members and guests of the LaFayette Study Club. Reporter Francis King described the event:

Since becoming a naturalized American citizen, Mrs. Newman, who won the prestigious NSDAR Americanism Award last spring, has told her story of tragedy and triumph to audiences across the country proudly and chides American-born citizens who use the flag-raising time at athletic events to get refreshments or talk. She carries with her the triangular-folded American flag that draped the casket of her husband, United States Army LTC Frank Charles Newman, killed on his second tour of duty in Vietnam.

Mrs. Newman says the flag is a "diploma," a call to duty. "If my husband could die for this country, I have an obligation to live for this country."

The story Mrs. Newman tells is one of almost continuous adversity that could have ended in despair. "I have survived because of prayer and the love of Jesus," she says. . .

"World War II was over, and the government had control of a co-op society. My father was told he was a capitalist. He walked into his bakery one day and someone else was seated behind his desk. They told him he owned too much.

"When the government tends toward collectivism and plays the role of a helping hand, it eventually owns you," she said.

That evening, Eva also shared her growing concerns about the fragile nature of freedom. Francis King's article continued:

She is deeply troubled about the erosion of freedoms in America. "I don't get involved in the big-time government; I'm not that smart," Mrs. Newman said, following the meeting. "If I knew all the answers, I would be in Washington, D.C. But I know enough to know that if people demand the government take care of them, they are giving up their liberty," she said.

"Liberty doesn't erode overnight. It's like the mustard seed Jesus mentioned in the Bible. It was so small you couldn't see it. It's the same with liberty and freedom. it is lost in little seeds, one at a time."

Mrs. Newman knows first-hand "what animals people can become when the spiritual dimension is taken away," she said in her speech. "For the first 14 years of my life, it was totally alien to me."

Restoring prayer to public schools is vital for children to develop spiritually as well as physically and mentally, Mrs. Newman believes. "We are giving young people the wrong message. As adults, we perform the rituals of praying before congressional sessions in Washington. Yet, we say, if we did that in class, someone might be offended."

"We need to balance that out. We have to allow that same privilege for our children, even if we do offend. The creator of our nation is also the creator of the world."

As freedom erodes, Mrs. Newman fears Americans might eventually lose every vestige of public prayer and acknowledgement of God in public life. "I am more conscious of losing freedom because I have lived under other systems. I am forever on watch for someone to take it away. It is my magnificent obsession."

Her obsession is not easy to quell. Stricken with cancer of the esophagus several years ago, Mrs. Newman lost half of her windpipe to surgery, leaving her unable to speak above a whisper. Physicians told her she would never regain her voice.

"In a year and a half, I got my voice back. The doctor said he had never seen anything like it. It was because of my will to rise above circumstances and determination to allow God to shape my life. I believe each life has a plan."

God's plan for her, speaking on patriotism and freedom, has been confirmed through her "red, white and blue dates," she said. Mrs. Newman was married on July 5. Her son Michael was born on Flag Day, also Sunday and Father's Day. Her son Steven died on Flag Day, and his brother Mike's birthday.

Eva saw the new dates as a sign she should continue speaking.

"Liberty and justice, treasure them dearly. It is my way of paying back the

nation that so graciously adopted us," she says. "Those of us who have lived without freedom must always treasure them dearly in our hearts and souls."

The next spring, in late April 1995, Eva returned to Prague—this time she was greeted with admiration and accolades.

The tiny woman with the powerful voice had flown to Prague at the invitation of the Czech Republic government, and the irony of the invitation was not lost on her. Eva stood, eyes shining, at the front of the room. She thought of her parents and wished they could have lived to share this moment, when their eldest daughter had come full circle, to celebrate the 50th anniversary of the end of World War II.

Today, on April 27, 1995, Eva Honolka Newman was both the guest of honor and the guest speaker, at the unveiling of a new exhibit for the Aviation Museum, in Prague-Belich, Czech Republic. Eva addressed the dignitaries with a message of celebration and hope.

Honorable Minister of Defense, Dr. Vilm Holan, Ladies, Gentlemen, and Special Guests.

On this special day of the meeting of the Minister of Defense, Dr Vilem Holan with Czech graduates of military schools and courses in the United States, I am honored to participate with you in this stirring and remarkable occasion; the opening of the new exposition celebrating the 50th anniversary of the end of World War II at the aviation museum here in Prague-Belich.

In my lifetime, I didn't think the day would come when I would see freedom banners spread across Eastern Europe like butterflies struggling in flight. Voices joined together, growing more confident with each step; energized by the magical word, freedom.

In 1951, our family went to the U.S.A. as refugees and immigrants from Czechoslovakia. We arrived there hungry, torn, scarred, and scared, but there was the promise of opportunity to follow happiness with hope.

To have the dignity of work.

To praise our God.

To have the freedom to Love our fellow human beings.

To be of SERVICE.

To appreciate life as it was given to us by a power beyond ourselves.

We are grateful to the nation that so graciously adopted us—the United States of America.

I work as the supervisor of Capitol receptionists and guides in Montgomery, Alabama. I have greeted and seen thousands of people from many countries, but not from the Czech Republic. It wasn't until 1992, when Maxwell Air Force Base received officers from the Czech Republic to study at the International Officers School, Squadron Officer School, Air Command and Staff College, and the Air War College.

These are bright, intelligent men; eager to learn and to take home valuable lessons of leadership, trustworthiness, patriotism, and history, to help them steer the fledgling new republic towards liberty and freedom with new ideas.

I pray that these bright minds will continue their quest for liberty; to pass on what they have learned so freedom can continue to flourish. We know that it won't be a good world for any of us until it becomes a good world for all of us.

Each one, teach one, and each ten, teach ten, that liberated people determine their own future.

Freedom is not just a choice or an opportunity; it is an obligation to respect the truth of our moral identity. We must meet that obligation and the sacrifices for freedom before we can claim its privileges and benefits.

I wish to convey to the Czech people how proud they should be of their military officers, for how diligently they are working, with much enthusiasm and energy, with willingness to learn new principles and concepts of liberty. They should be given every opportunity to teach others and to share the lessons learned, so that the Czech Nation can reach new heights of a good life that it so rightly deserves.

During this valuable opening ceremony of the new Exposition of the Aviation Museum, I am returning to the Czech people, medals, memorabilia, and uniforms of a U.S. Army Master Aviator: a "Mustang" Officer who worked himself through the ranks of the military—Lt. Colonel Frank Charles Newman.

The gift Eva presented was significant for many reasons, including the fact that Frank was the only Czechoslovakia-born citizen to serve for the United States in the Vietnam War. It was rare for a naturalized American citizen, or one never going to military academy, to rise to the level of an officer. Frank accomplished that goal, as well.

Frank was born in Nepomuk, Czechoslovakia. he lived amidst fear of the second World War and later in fear of the oppression of Communism.

He came to the U.S. with a lot of hope and a lot of aspiration in his heart, but with very little else. Through long days and hard work, he gained his American Citizenship.

He enlisted in the U.S. Army, in Germany. He worked himself through the ranks, from a Private (E-1) to become a Commissioned Officer, and to the rank of Lt. Colonel (O-5) in 17 years. He was Commanding Officer of the 101st Aviation Company when he was killed.

I say that with a great deal of pride for our nation—the U.S.A.—because the promise of opportunity was fulfilled again when a man was given the chance to follow happiness with hope.

Frank was my better half, my partner in life, and the father of our children. Five days before he was scheduled to go home from his second tour of duty in Vietnam, he lost his life there. I became a widow, with three little children, two boys and a girl, and when the time came, I pinned Frank's wings on my son's chest and I was proud to be the wife of a soldier who gave his all!

Frank's ultimate dream was to see the Czech people free; to have democracy as once experienced for 20 years under President Tomas Garique Masarik. Frank was a son of two nations; he never forgot his homeland, and he was also faithful to the nation that adopted him.

Because of his love of the Czech people, I feel it is appropriate, and I feel very grateful that his humble possessions will be part of this museum. We can start building bridges of respect and admiration—one nation to another, join hands as brothers and sisters and walk in peace on this place called "Earth." Memories are not just imprints of the past upon us—they are the keeper of what is meaningful for our deepest hopes and dreams.

The next month, on May 29, 1995, twenty-five years after Frank's death, the *Montgomery Advertiser* again published a story about Eva Honolka Newman and her commitment to speaking about patriotism, God and family.

The writer, Frank Mastin, Jr., told of Eva's visit to her husband's grave in Ozark, Alabama, that Memorial Day.

"If LTC Frank Charles Newman is looking down from heaven this Memorial Day, he must be pleased to see that his widow, Eva, has dedicated his life to keeping his memory and spirit alive," he wrote.

The story told of Frank Newman's career, the arranged marriage between the two displaced persons camp survivors, and the love that grew between them.

"Basically, Frank Newman made me who I am today," Eva said in the article. She explained that was propelled into the speaking circuit by a series of occurrences in her life. The article summarized those events:

"I know the Lord has a mission for my life," Mr. Newman said, "and my mission just happens to be red, white and blue—God, duty, honor and country.

"I feel like wherever my husband quit his mission, it was given to me to pick it up and carry it on."

Eva was one of only a few naturalized American citizens to be awarded the Americanism Medal from the Daughters of the American Revolution. Here, she poses wearing the medal.

CHAPTER THIRTY-THREE

A SPECIAL PERSON

During the years of 2001-2014, Eva continued to make a difference in the lives of those she touched, whether they were members of her extended family, or others she met along the way. She owned a triplex and often provided one of the apartments, rent-free to visitors from the Czech Republic, or students attending college at Auburn University in Alabama. Many told stories of her hospitality and spirited conversations.

From one of her nephews:

"Aunt Eva was special. She was fun, sweet, loving and always the life of the parties. Her presence was contagious and always made everyone smile. I will never forget in 2001 at the family reunion in Alabama, she was a little stressed one day. She asked me if I wanted to see Montgomery history with her, and of course I thought that would be cool. We started and ended up at a brewery.

She told me she needed that time away and thanked me for hanging out with her. We had a blast. "

From a male friend from Kosovo, Arbin Skivjani, who lived with Eva while attending Auburn University, AL, in 2002:

"The moment I saw her, it felt like I had known her for ages—such a beautiful soul. For those 18 or so years that I knew Eva, she was like a second mother to me, always giving, never asking for anything in return."

From a male friend from the Czech Republic, Patrica Ricica, who lived with her while looking for employment:

"I met Eva in Montgomery in 2003 or 2004. My friend came to town for a visit, so I showed him around downtown and we walked by the First White House of the Confederacy where she worked. The place looked closed, so we walked past it. And then, it was like something stopped me. So I looked over my shoulder and then walked back to the front door and opened it. My friend walked back too. So we looked around, speaking in Czech language, saying silly things and then there she was in her little gift shop. Just listening to us. She didn't say anything until we were about to leave, and she shocked us by talking to us in the Czech language as well. 'Let me know if you have any questions, boys.' She invited us home later for a cup of tea and we apologized for some of the things we said about her museum. I will never forget the feeling inside when I walked back to her museum. Destiny's call for sure. She was like a mother to me."

From a niece:
"She had the most beautiful blue eyes that sparkled and a smile and laugh that was contagious. Her hugs made you feel warm and loved. She had a gift of lifting everyone up around her. Despite all the obstacles and tragedies in her life, she still saw the good in everyone and everything. She was always positive. She was a strong, courageous and beautiful person inside and out."

Eva always had time to welcome people into her home. She sponsored many international officers stationed at Maxwell Air Force Base. She supported Girls State, Boys State, and the Hugh O'Brian Foundation. Dedicated to serving others, she continued this tradition well into her late seventies.

In 2002, at 64, Eva became a Goodwill Ambassador, as part of a program created by the International Officers School at Air University that supports international officers and their families while they were attending school at Maxwell Air Force Base. Over the next nine years (through 2011) Eva sponsored 55 Czech Republic International Officer School students and some of their families.

Eva was recognized for her love and loyalty to her country through the work she did at IOS, but she never forgot the blood and tears that went into immigrating to America, and the chance of a new life that it gave her.

The Czech officers she took into her home were struck by her kindness and her sense of humor.

"I try to teach them—don't do this, do this," Eva once said. "Like a mother would."

"When they first arrive, they say to me, 'There's a church on every corner. But where are the pubs?'"

"And so we begin with our discussions."

"I bring them here, as if they were at home. To the same kind of food, maybe. And we talk about the Czech Republic, and then we start to compare the way things are done in each country. And they ask, why do we do it this way? And, when they understand, perhaps they become better people than they were when they came."

Eva infused so much laughter into her lessons for the officers that they easily accepted her suggestions. It wasn't unusual for them to find small ways to please her. On one occasion, she arrived at the White House of the Confederacy to see a special poster welcoming her:

Honorary Colonels Of Alabama

Robert Zobac And Jaroslav Morochovic

Have Awarded

EVA HONOLKA NEWMAN

The Title Of

THE MOTHER OF CZECH AIR FORCE OFFICERS.

Eva embraced her role as a mentor and spokesperson for young people. In 2002, she attended the unveiling of a new exhibit at The American Village in Montevallo, Alabama, where she was one of eight Americans featured. *The Shelby County Reporter* wrote: "The Voting Experience, located in the

Village's historic Colonial Courthouse, traces the history of the right to vote from the bridge in Lexington, VA, during the American Revolution to a Czechoslovakian immigrant's tireless work to encourage Americans to not take for granted freedoms many across the world go without."

The narrator introduced Eva as the supervisor of Capital Receptionists in Montgomery. He told of her immigration to the United States with her family and noted that she had survived the loss of four sons, a husband killed in Vietnam and cancer. "But," he said, "she loves her adopted country."

When the exhibit light shone on Eva's portrait, a recording of her voice challenged the audience: "Ask yourselves, how many times have you failed to exercise your right to vote? Voting every time there is an election, this is a crying need of America…When we vote, we help America fulfill her destiny."

The American Village continued the exhibit for several years. Eva returned in 2004 for a special presentation to the Madison County School System. Her appearances represented her ongoing commitment to sharing the importance of freedom, and her gratitude to the United States of America.

During one of her speeches in 2006, Eva spoke proudly about her mother, Jarmila:

As children, we grasped and stumbled, and the only emotion we had was fear. Fear of bombings, hunger, and all the atrocities that came with war. My mother's protective faith guided us beyond the darkness of the difficult years and we saw the sky of everlasting glory and the light of God.

In 1948, we escaped from the oppressive Communist government. As the night came, we left our homeland. The path was dark; we shook with cold and fear, but Mom drew us close and covered us with her coat. She was near and no harm could come to us.

The next day we walked far; we grew weary, but Mother cheered us on. "Be brave. Soon we will be there." When we reached the borders of two countries, we realized we could not have done it without Mother. She taught us courage, fortitude in the face of harshness, strength to persevere, and faith in God. She taught us to stay frugal, not waste anything, and to share with others.

In 1951, Mom came to the United States of America with my father and their five children. As a refugee, she dreamed of a life founded on new values, free of the myths of the Old World. The aspiration of a better life had an inner direction founded on the urge for the good and the true of this country…Mom studied the Constitution and the laws of the land. She cheered us on to learn the new English language so we could become good citizens. She was a patriot.

The years passed; she grew old, but her children were tall and strong. We walked with courage, faith, perseverance and loyalty to our new country. Mother said, "I know the end of my journey is better than the beginning, for my children can walk alone. Their children after them can enjoy freedom and walk with God's blessings."

I can no longer see my mother, but she is always with me. She is a living presence. She lives in my laughter. She is crystallized in every teardrop. She is the smell of bleach in freshly laundered socks. She is the whisper of the leaves as I walk down the street. My mom is the map I follow with every step I take.

When I think of her, I remember Proverbs 31:25-26 ESV Strength and dignity are her clothing, and she laughs at the time to come. She opens her mouth with wisdom, and the teaching of kindness is on her tongue.

It was with sadness that Eva and her family learned the Amana Bakery her father had worked so hard to build had ended. The bakery closed permanently in 2013. The staff had dwindled to six by then. It never reopened to the public again.

That January, Patricia received a phone call from a family friend in Cedar Rapids, Attorney Walter McNamara. He had read the article about the bakery closing, "Last Loaves," in a statewide newspaper. The article's distortion of history shocked McNamara; it omitted any mention of John, who had built the bakery to its highest levels. Eva and her family were stunned by the omission.

The business their father had built into a successful regional company had steadily declined since his departure. Although it had been nearly 38 years since John Honolka retired from that business, Eva had not forgotten the impact he had made during nearly two decades of management, from 1955 to 1975. She remembered the day the bank refused to lend him the money to purchase the bakery, and her father's determination to grow the business—and the profits. She had saved the 1966 magazine article from *Bakery Production and Marketing* magazine, where reporters attributed a 1000% sales growth over the past 11 years to her father's innovations and leadership.

With so much written evidence of John Honolka's contributions to the bakery, Eva was disappointed to see the newspaper had ignored her father's role in the history of the business. Instead, the entire article gave credit to others whose patriarch had begun his career at the bakery in 1960 as assistant to the dough maker, learning under John Honolka, during those years when the bakery grew exponentially. The glory years were not mentioned in the story—only the patriarch who worked his way up to take over as manager in 1974, shortly before John Honolka retired, leaving behind a thriving regional bakery.

Granted, the patriarch and his extended family—ending with his daughter—ran the bakery from 1975 until it closed its doors in 2013, just under four decades. But, in its entire history, the biggest growth years were the two decades where the bakery was in John Honolka's capable hands. Omitting this part of the history stung the Honolka family, and many others. With the encouragement of their attorney, four of the adult children—along with family friends—wrote letters to the newspaper asking them to correct the article.

On February 5, 2013, Eva sent an impassioned letter to the reporter who wrote the article imploring him to acknowledge her father's contributions to the bakery. She wrote of John Honolka as a visionary who was always ahead of his time—with new ideas, inventions, and workflow improvements. She described his passion for business and entrepreneurship, and told of his dream of building a business in America.

Eva explained her father's background as a professional athlete in

Czechoslovakia, where he served as both an athlete and a team manager, and where he developed a philosophy balancing body, will and mind. She noted his commitment to culture, education, and a peaceful society.

In a few short paragraphs, Eva provided an account of her father's attempt to buy the bakery, his failure to obtain a bank loan, his subsequent success managing the business, and his desire to take the bakery national—a request the Amana Society denied.

They waited.

On April 3, 2013, the family aimed higher. They wrote to the newspaper's editor and sent copies to the publisher, the Iowa Governor, and Cedar Rapids attorney, Walter McNamara. They enclosed the article from the September 24, 1966, issue of *Bakery Production and Marketing* magazine which profiled John Honolka's contributions to the growth of the bakery.

They noted the reporter's incomplete article and requested the newspaper correct the discrepancies.

My brother Don and my sister Eva have both contacted the reporter of the article "Last Loves," explaining the discrepancy and injustice. There has been no reply or acknowledgement.

My sister Patricia and I now direct this discrepancy and injustice to all recipients above and all of the siblings of one John Honolka. The integrity of actual people, history and events are at stake, along with the integrity of the newspaper.

This letter, signed by Thomas and his sister Patricia, also listed contact information for their three siblings—Eva, Lada (Don), and John Jr. They concluded:

We, the children of one John Honolka, would be glad to provide information to AMEND AND FACTUALLY report the history of the Amana Society Bakery and restore the integrity of history and the newspaper.

Again, there was no response. Not a note. Not a phone call. Not a retraction or a clarification in the publication. Ironically, the newspaper's "Corrections" policy appeared on the back side of the original clipping of the

"Last Loaves" article. Clearly, it did not promise an action, but it implied that the publication cared about accuracy and fairness:

The newspaper strives for accuracy and fairness. Errors in our news columns will be corrected in the section where the article appeared. Readers who believe the paper has erred may request a correction by calling (515) 284-8065.

At one point, Tommy emailed the reporter and arranged a face-to-face meeting. He explained the true story of the bakery's history, as well as the individual who made it a success: John Honolka. Tommy showed the reporter a newspaper article from 1955, telling of his father's position as the manager of the bakery. He shared the 1966 article from the national industry magazine praising John Honolka's leadership and innovations. And, he played a 1963 DVD of a 4-minute interview featuring John Honolka in a television special about the Amana Colonies.

Although the reporter suggested that he might do a follow up article after John's death—or within a larger story on the history of Iowa—neither ever happened. Patricia talked with the reporter a few months afterward and asked if it was too late to make the corrections. He agreed it could potentially be done, but he declined to do it.

Ultimately, the family took the high road. They were disappointed that their many letters were ignored. But they were more concerned that newspaper accounts are all-to-often the only history surviving generations. They knew the truth of their father's impact on the bakery. His story was well documented in a nationally respected industry magazine. Together, they had made a valiant effort to set the record straight.

It was apparent the Iowa newspaper had no interest in the accuracy they professed to protect or felt the history they had omitted was unimportant. Perhaps the news article wasn't worth their continued frustration. After all, they had fought far bigger battles in their lifetimes.

The Honolka five, at a family reunion in 2001. From left: Don, Johnny, Eva, Vlasta, and Tom.

CHAPTER THIRTY-FOUR

LIVING IN THE SPOTLIGHT

It was Wednesday, August 19, 2015. Once again, Eva was to be recognized for her life's work—but this time her homeland presented the award. She was 78, and held her head high, just as she had when she faced the Hungarian border guards at age eleven.

Her vivid blue eyes glowed with the same passion; her blond curls were now a halo of silver.

The Montgomery, Alabama weather was typical for August—a stifling 86 degrees, steeped in humidity—as dignitaries arrived at Maxwell Air Force Base to recognize Eva Honolka Newman. The small gathering of family, friends, and military officers watched as she moved slowly to the center of the stage.

Calm and composed, Eva clasped her hands in front of her and waited.

She wore a stylish navy-blue suit; an American flag scarf added a touch of patriotic color. She gazed into the audience and found the faces that made her smile: her daughter Julie; son Michael and his wife; and, of course, Brigadier General Chris "Boots" Coffelt, commander of the Air War College, who beamed with pride.

Col. Michael Peterson, head of the International Officers School, as well as current Czech students Col. Cepelka and Major Josef Korinek stood near them.

Brigadier General Jiri Verner, from the Defense, Military and Air Attache of the Czech Republic, stepped to the microphone. He had flown from Prague to meet this woman, and to bestow one of his country's highest honors upon her.

Brigadier General Jiri Verner, Defense Military and Air Attache of the Czech Republic, decorates Mrs. Eva Honolka Newman.

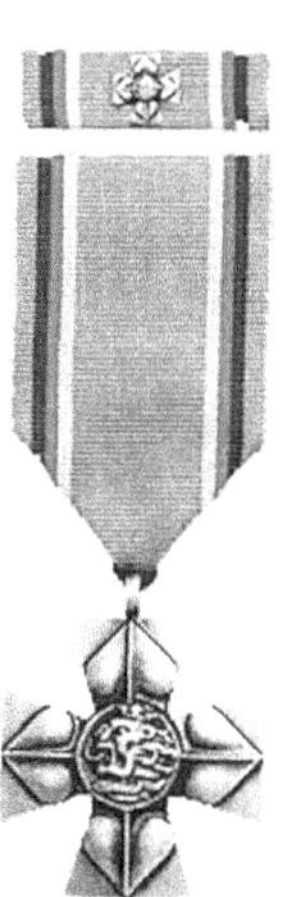

Eva Honolka Newman was awarded with the Cross of Merit of the Czech Minister of Defense 3rd Class, for her significant contributions in the development of the Ministry of Defense of the Czech Republic. The ceremony took place on August 19, 2015, at the Maxwell Air Force base in Montgomery, Alabama.

Holding the rare medallion before him, Brigadier General Verner displayed it for the audience. The boxed medallion was suspended from a light green ribbon, striped with thin lines of green, blue, red, and white on either side. One face of the medal depicted the head of a lion, as found on the Czech coat of arms. The reverse side contained a Spanish shield divided in half. The upper field featured the crowned Czech lion, in the lower field held two crossed swords.

"While this cross is often presented to recognize heroism, leadership during combat, and for noteworthy service in combat activities, the Minister of Defense may also present the cross to citizens of foreign nations," Brigadier General Verner said. "The conditions for the award are for notably serving in cooperation with the Defense department, supporting combat readiness in the Czech military, and for activities in support of the Armed Forces of the Czech Republic."

He held the box higher, for the audience to see.

"Ladies and gentlemen, and distinguished guests. It is my pleasure to award Eva Honolka Newman with the Cross of Merit of the Czech Minister of Defense, third class, for her significant contributions in the development of the Ministry of Defense of the Czech Republic."

Lifting the medal from its velvet box, Brigadier General Verner approached Eva.

"May I?"

Eva's eyes crinkled with her smile. "Yes."

Verner pinned the bronze cross onto Eva's jacket, just above her heart.

As a beam of light sparked from the medal, the audience burst into applause.

Eva remained, a small figure in the center of the stage. The brave young girl who had fled Communism so long ago was still alive within the seventy-eight-year-old grandmother who graced the spotlight. This petite woman, with her quiet strength and melodic Czech accent, had served as the voice of freedom for two countries, spanning nearly eight decades.

She spoke confidently from the podium, repeating the message she never tired of sharing.

"We gave everything. We gave our heritage. We gave our language. We gave everything, for an intangible called freedom, that this nation gave us."

Her blue eyes blazed with passion.

"It is my utmost obligation—till I take my last breath—to pay back to a nation that so graciously adopted us."

Eva Honolka Newman spent her entire life championing the cause of freedom. The Cross of Merit represented an acknowledgement of her efforts; from the homeland she never abandoned.

Three years later, in March 2018, when her health began to fail, Eva moved into an independent senior living community near her daughter in Alabama. Her beloved cat, Whisky, came along. Like an obedient puppy, the cat trailed Eva into the dining room every day, where he enjoyed the company of others. Occasionally, Whisky spent a few hours away from Eva, visiting neighboring apartments where he allowed the residents to stroke his fur and scratch beneath his chin. Soon, the word was out: everyone loved Whisky.

Sometimes, when she closed her eyes to doze in her favorite chair, snapshots of Eva's life played against her lids: she danced in a field of dandelions, cried as a Russian soldier beat his horse. She remembered children playing. Children dying. Chip playing his trumpet. Her musings always concluded with the same two images: the American flag draped over a coffin, and a bronze cross gleaming in the sunlight.

In the spring of 2019, Eva reflected on the journey of her life.

How strange that, after eighty-two years of my life, I feel the urge to share the journey that was my kaleidoscope of experiences, or as I say, 'my lot in life.'

By God's grace, I have risen above the trepidation, the pain of separation from one's homeland, the loss of identity when caught up in the upheavals of governments wanting to own your heart and soul, that chain you to the yoke of mental slavery.

My lot in life was to 'accept the things I could not change' realizing that I came with nothing into this world, and that I would leave not taking anything with me but with God's blessings I would come to the end of my journey with total victory.

Everything in between—family, children, personal possessions—will be a gift from God, loaned to me for my life. Under all circumstances, I thank my heavenly Father for all that He gives me. Good or bad. For, 'Greater is He who is in me, than he who is in the world.'

I write these pages with great affection for this nation called America, that so generously adopted me and took our family out of the mire and despair, with the promise to pursue happiness and hope. We realized that we must bring happiness to life ourselves, and with the undergirding of God, we will be successful.

I have always felt that it is a must to pay back to this Nation that so graciously adopted us, and our Heavenly Father who guided us.

With great purpose, we studied the Constitution and the Bill of Rights. We were law abiding citizens. We learned the English language and understood the great privilege of voting.

"Give me liberty or give me death." The words of Patrick Henry became our motto, and yes, we joined the military to protect the precious liberty and this way of life. We became God fearing, law-abiding United States of America citizens.

A few months later, on July 8, 2019, Eva suffered a stroke. Facing an illness of her own, Eva's sister Patricia could not leave Kansas. The two sisters missed their daily phone conversations, which had become a mixture of Czech and English. The slang from both languages resulted in frequent laughter, with the sisters occasionally imitating the words and accents of their parents—as though they had no accents of their own. Later, Patricia referred to this as one of the worst years of her life. Both sisters were ill. One died.

On September 13, 2020, death silenced Eva Honolka Newman's voice. She was 83.

Her campaign for freedom lives on.

EPILOGUE

In October 2022, Eva Honolka Newman and Frank Newman were each posthumously presented with the highest medals of honor available from their native country, in recognition of their contributions to freedom. The Czech Republic Minister of Defence awarded Frank the *State Defence Cross of Merit* (gold)*, and Eva the *Golden Linden Medal.***

The medals were presented to the Newman's daughter, Julie, who traveled to Washington, D.C. to accept the award on behalf of her parents. Later, she donated the medals to the National Czech & Slovak Museum & Library in Cedar Rapids, Iowa, where they remain today.

*State Defence Cross: Minister of Defence of the Czech Republic awards the decoration only rarely and especially to soldiers and other citizens of the Czech Republic and foreign nationals for heroism in combat, excellent command role in combat or to those who made their best in defence of the Czech Republic and its constitutional order especially when putting their health or lives at risk, who saved human lives or high values of Czech Republic´s property, regardless if done on the Czech territory or outside.

The State Defence Cross has a one grade, and it can be awarded repeatedly.

The decoration is awarded together with a certificate with rank, title, first and family name of the awarded person and a serial number. The certificate is signed by the Minister of Defence of the Czech Republic.

MINISTRYNĚ OBRANY

uděluje

KŘÍŽ OBRANY STÁTU
in memoriam

**podplukovník (Lt. Col.)
Frank C. NEWMAN**

Ministryně obrany ČR

Číslo: 267   13. října 2022

DECREE
(on personal affairs)

The Minister of Defense of the Czech Republic issues the present decree on personal affairs:

In accordance with the provisions under Article 5 of the Order of the Minister No. 40/2017 of the MoD Bulletin, the Military Decorations, and Article 1, 2 and 3 of Annex 1 to the about-mentioned Order, as of October 13th, 2022.

For valor, heroism and selflessness in the fight for freedom and democracy.

The State Defense Cross of the Minister of Defense of the Czech Republic, No. 267

is awarded in memoriam to

Lieutenant Colonel Frank C. Newman
July 5th, 1927 - February 24th, 1970.

The Czechoslovakian State Defence Cross of Merit awarded to Frank Newman, posthumously, in 2022. LTC Frank Charles Newman is honored on Panel 13W, Line 51, on the Vietnam Veterans Memorial in Washington, D.C. He was the only Czech-born citizen to serve for the U.S. in Vietnam.

MINISTRYNĚ OBRANY

uděluje

VYZNAMENÁNÍ ZLATÉ LÍPY

in memoriam

Eva HONOLKA NEWMAN

13. října 2022

Ministryně obrany ČR

Číslo 312

DECREE
(on personal affairs)

The Minister of Defense of the Czech Republic issues the present decree on personal affairs:

In accordance with the provisions under Article 5 of the Order of the Minister No. 40/2017 of the MoD Bulletin, the Military Decorations, and Article 9 of Annex 1 to the about-mentioned Order, as of October 13th, 2022.

For a long-standing support of Czech military students in the USA.

The Decoration of Golden Linden of the Minister of Defense of the Czech Republic, No. 312

is awarded in memoriam to

Ms. Eva Honolka Newman
May 14th, 1937 - September 13th, 2020

The Golden Linden Medal from the Czechoslovakian State Defence Department, awarded to Eva Honolka Newman, posthumously in 2022.

**Golden Linden Medal: Minister of Defence awards this decoration only in rare cases to citizens of the Czech Republic and foreign nationals, who highly contributed to defence of human rights and freedoms, especially to those, who saved human life, health and property, to people, who exceptionally contributed to protection of basic principles of democratic state and the state of law or contributed to development of defence and security of the Czech Republic, including scientific and professional work. The decoration has a one grade and can be awarded repeatedly.

The Golden Linden Decoration is awarded together with a certificate with rank, title, first and family name of the awarded person and a serial number. The certificate is signed by the Minister of Defence of the Czech Republic.

After his death in 1970, LTC Newman was awarded several medals for the period of October 1969 to February 1970, while he served in Vietnam as commanding officer, 131st Aviation Company, 212th Combat Aviation Battalion, 1st Aviation Brigade. These were presented to Eva and her children:

The Legion of Merit
The Distinguished Flying Cross,
The Bronze Star Medal
The Purple Heart
The Air Medal with 19 Oak Leaf Clusters

During his military service, Frank Charles Newman also received additional medals, including:

Aviator Badge (Master)
Two Air Medals
National Defense Services Medal
Republic of Vietnam Campaign Medal
Army Presidential Unit Citation
Vietnam Service Medal

SIBLINGS:

Vladimir "Lada" Donald Honolka had four sons and a daughter. Don was a successful businessman in Iowa, where he was an independent distributor of bakery products in the quad cities. He moved to Texas, where he spent many years in the automobile industry. Later, he founded Honolka Distribution, successfully distributing beef jerky products. He and his wife, Sharon, live in Springtown, Texas.

Vlasta "Patricia" Honolka married and had two sons. She moved to Kansas, where she worked as a registered nurse for 36 years in hospitals. She still lives in Kansas.

John Honolka, Jr. spent 40 successful years in the automobile industry—working long hours, including nights and weekends. He built a loyal customer base, sold hundreds of vehicles, and spent many years in sales manager positions at various automobile dealerships. He and his wife Sandra were married for 51 years. They had two children and four grandchildren. John died on November 11, 2020, ten weeks after Eva's death. Sandra still lives in Justin, Texas.

Thomas Honolka spent his formative years in Iowa, going to school and working for the bakery where he mastered every workspace. In 1970, at the age of 20, he moved to Texas and He worked for multiple Fortune 500 Food companies, including positions as district or regional manager. For the last 20 years of his career, Tom was a market manager for a national bakery supply firm. He retired in 2019 and moved to Arkansas in 2020. He and his wife, Leslie, raised five children.

EVA'S CHILDREN:

Michael David Newman became an electrical engineer. He married and had two daughters. Michael died January 17, 2022, at 62.

Julie Ann Newman married, started her own housekeeping business, and had three children. She lives in Hoover, Alabama.

ACKNOWLEDGEMENTS

No amount of thank you will ever be enough to recognize those who gave selflessly for the welfare of others.

Many good people live among evil. Let's not judge a country or nationality by the evil that represents them but remember the good people they oppress and overshadow.

Many strangers helped us immeasurably along the way. I will always remember The prison guard (name unknown) who smuggled us aspirins in prison, possibly saving two-year-old Johnny's life; the conductor (name unknown) who conveniently pretended not to see us on his train, preventing us from being imprisoned again; the farmer (name unknown) who risked his life to hide and transport us in his hay wagon on our unknown journey.

In America, we found a country that accepted us and gave us the luxury of freedom. Our thanks go to the farmer who sponsored us, and to the farm families in Protivin, Iowa, who brought us food or invited us for a meal. We owe a debt of gratitude to Mr. and Mrs. Milo Naxera, from Cedar Rapids, Iowa, who found a house for our family in Walford, Iowa. Later, Mr. and Mrs. Andrew Polehna gave my father a job in Cedar Rapids, Iowa. Being a butcher was far from the baking business he knew, but so was farming, and my father appreciated the opportunity to earn a living.

I am forever grateful to the family we left behind: My maternal grandparents, Rudolph and Marie Kralik, my aunt, and my uncle, were good, kind people who were brutally treated and persecuted because they refused to join the Communist Party. They were all punished because we escaped.

Also, I thank my parents, John and Jarmila, who had the courage to refuse to be puppets of the Communist regime. The pair that "gave up all, for freedom," paid a steep price to enhance their children's lives. And, of course, my sister Eva, who always felt this story should be told. For many years, she tirelessly gave free lectures to churches, schools, universities, clubs, and political groups on the importance of freedom and voting.

All are in God's care now, but not forgotten on earth.

Not to be forgotten, a big thank you also goes to kind, talented hardworking Susan Armstrong, who listened to me patiently, never complained, criticized or judged, as I rambled on. If there was an issue, it was solved in a polite, constructive manner, just like the lady she is.

For all these acts of kindness, and many others too numerous to mention, my heart is full. I hope "They Gave All, For Freedom" will touch your heart as well.

May freedom ring, always and forever, in the United States of America.

–Vlasta Honolka

In Gratitude

The authors wish to thank those who assisted in proofreading, editing, formatting and publishing of this book. Special thanks to LaRue K. Gillespie, reader and advisor.

Our deepest gratitude to the team at AC Strategic Marketing, especially Belinda Atteberry, Kristen Nuss and Miho Halscy. Your creative vision and attention to detail turned this book into a work of art. Thank you for going above and beyond our expectations. We appreciate each of you.

–Susan Trout Armstrong & Vlasta Honolka

ENDNOTES

i Bureau of European and Eurasian Affairs, "U.S. Relations With the Czech Republic," U.S. Department of State, April 6, 2021. https://www.state.gov/u-s-relations-with-the-czech-republic/

ii The Editors of Encyclopaedia Britannica, "History & Society: Konrad Henlein, Sudeten-German Politician," Britannica, May 6, 2023. https://www.britannica.com/biography/Konrad-Henlein

iii The Editors of Encyclopaedia Britannica, "Geography & Travel: Sudetenland: Historical Region, Europe," Britannica, August 25, 2023. https://www.britannica.com/place/Sudetenland

iv Holocaust-Era Assets, "RG 84: Germany: State Department and Foreign Affairs Records," The U.S. National Archives & Records Administration, August 15, 2016. https://www.archives.gov/research/holocaust/finding-aid/civilian/rg-84-germany.html

v The Holocaust Explained, "Planning for War: The Hossbach Memorandum," The Wiener Holocaust Library, 2016. https://www.theholocaustexplained.org/life-in-nazi-occupied-europe/foreign-policy-and-the-road-to-war/planning-for-war-the-hossbach-memorandum/

vi United States Holocaust Memorial Museum, "Nazi Territorial Aggression: The Anschluss," Holocaust Encyclopedia, 2023. https://encyclopedia.ushmm.org/content/en/article/nazi-territorial-aggression-the-anschluss vii Skene, Gordon, "March 11, 1938: The Word is Anschluss," Past Daily: A Sound Archive of News, History, Music, March 2022. https://pastdaily.com/2022/03/11/march-11-1938-the-word-is-anschluss-germany-annexes-austria-german-troops-in-vienna/

viii Chornyl, Maxim, "Hitler in Vienna 1938: Anschluss of Austria," War Documentary: Travel Your Own History, Published March 5, 2018, Updated October 3, 2023. https://war-documentary.info/anschluss-of-austria-1938/

ix Holocaust-Era Assets, "RG 84: Czechoslovakia: State Department and Foreign Affairs Records," The U.S. National Archives & Records Administration, August 15, 2016. https://www.archives.gov/research/holocaust/finding-aid/civilian/rg-84-czech.html

x Burns, Tracy A., "Life During the Nazi Occupation," Private Prague Guide Custom Travel Services, 2023. https://www.private-prague-guide.com/article/life-during-the-nazi-occupation/

xi Beyond Prague, "Made in the Czech Republic-Tatra," The Czech Republic, Outside of the Capital, 2023. https://beyondprague.net/made-in-the-czech-republic/made-in-the-czech-republic-tatra/

xii Burns, Tracy A., "Life During the Nazi Occupation," Private Prague Guide Custom Travel Services, 2023. https://www.private-prague-guide.com/article/life-during-the-nazi-occupation/

xiii Bryant, Chad Carl, "Heydrich Imposes Racial Order," Prague In Black: Nazi Rule and Czech Nationalism, (USA: First Harvard University Press, 2009), Chapter 4.

xiv Deac, Wil, "The Assassination of Reinhard Heydrich, The Butcher of Prague," Warfare History Network, 2023. https://warfarehistorynetwork.com/the-assassination-of-reinhard-heydrich-the-butcher-of-prague/

xv Brendel, Toni, "Lidice, Remembered Around the World," Penfield Books, 2013. Pages 15-16.

xvi Beyond Prague, "Made in the Czech Republic-Tatra," The Czech Republic, Outside of the Capital, 2023. https://beyondprague.net/made-in-the-czech-republic/made-in-the-czech-republic-tatra/

xvii Rajcan, Vanda, "The Slovak National uprising of 1944," The National WWII Museum, Sept. 12, 2023. https://www.nationalww2museum.org/war/articles/slovak-national-uprising-1944

xviii Burns, Tracy A., "Life During the Nazi Occupation," Private Prague Guide Custom Travel Services, 2023. https://www.private-prague-guide.com/article/life-during-the-nazi-occupation/

xix Gentry, Connie, "Calling All Czechs! The Prague Uprising of 1945," The National WWII Museum, May 5, 2020. https://www.nationalww2museum.org/war/articles/prague-uprising-1945

xx Burns, Tracy A., "Life During the Nazi Occupation," Private Prague Guide Custom Travel Services, 2023. https://www.private-prague-guide.com/article/life-during-the-nazi-occupation/

xxi Haskett, Norm, "Czech Head Tells German Minority to Go Home," The Daily Chronicles of WWII, 2023. https://ww2days.com/dev1/czech-head-tells-german-minority-to-go-home.html

xxii Burns, Tracy A., "Edvard Benes-Czechoslovak Statesman," Private Prague Guide Custom Travel Services, 2023. https://www.private-prague-guide.com/article/edvard-benes/

xxiii Horalikova, Dana, "Communism in Czechoslovakia," Prague Behind the Scenes, August 18, 2022. https://www.praguebehindthescenes.com/Communism-in-czechoslovakia

xxiv Burns, Tracy A., "Life During the Communist Era in Czechoslovakia," Prague Behind the Scenes, 2023. https://www.private-prague-guide.com/article/life-during-the-Communist-era-in-czechoslovakia/

xxv Britannica, The Editors of Encyclopaedia. "International Refugee Organization". Encyclopedia Britannica, 2 Mar. 2012. https://www.britannica.com/topic/International-Refugee-Organization-historical-UN-agency. https://www.britannica.com/topic/International-Refugee-Organization-historical-UN-agency

xxvi Woolley, John, and Peters, Gerhard, "The American Presidency Project," UC Santa Barbara, May 12, 2012. https://www.presidency.ucsb.edu/statistics/elections/1952

xxvii Freeman, Tyson, "The 1950s: Post-War America Hitches Up and Heads for the 'Burbs," CRE Business News, WealthManagement.com, September 30, 1999. https://www.wealthmanagement.com/news/1950s-post-war-america-hitches-and-heads-burbs

xxviii Reeves, Thomas C, "Dwight D. Eisenhower," Britannica, October 31, 2023. https://www.britannica.com/biography/Dwight-D-Eisenhower

xxix "History of the Seven Villages," Amana Colonies, 2023. https://amanacolonies.com/visitors-guide/history-of-the-seven-villages/

xxx "When Was Sliced Bread Invented?" Blog Article, Gold medal Bakery, May 28, 2021. https://www.goldmedalbakery.com/blog/when-was-sliced-bread-invented/

"History of Sliced Bread – Modern Baking Industry," History of Bread, 2023. http://www.historyofbread.com/bread-history/history-of-sliced-bread/#:~:text=Then%20the%20sliced%20bread%20appeared,whole%20loaf%20at%20a%20time.

xxxi Kline, Jim, "Many Choices for Packaging Film," Baking Business.com, December, 2016. https://www.bakingbusiness.com/articles/45110-many-choices-for-packaging-film

xxxii Hinsley, Nana, "The History of Polyethylene," Global Plastic Sheeting, February 13, 2015. https://www.globalplasticsheeting.com/our-blog-resource-library/bid/23095/the-history-of-polyethylene

xxxiii "Week of October 1," The United States of America Vietnam War Commemoration, 2015. https://www.vietnamwar50th.com/education/week_of_october_1/#:~:text=On%20October%201%2C%201965%E2%80%94exactly,new%20approach%20to%20infantry%20tactics.

xxxiv "U.S. Troop Levels in Vietnam," The Vietnam War: Interpreting Statistics, Digital History, 2021. https://www.digitalhistory.uh.edu/disp_textbook.cfm?smtID=11&psid=3844

xxxv "What Happened in 1966, Important News and Events," The People History Home, 2023. https://www.thepeoplehistory.com/1966.html

xxxvi History.Com editors, "Vietnam War Protests," History, November 1, 2022. https://www.history.com/topics/vietnam-war/vietnam-war-protests

xxxvii The Editors of Encyclopaedia Britannica, "Velvet Revolution, Czechoslovakian History," Britannica, September 26, 2023. https://www.britannica.com/topic/Velvet-Revolution

www.ingramcontent.com/pod-product-compliance
Lightning Source LLC
Chambersburg PA
CBHW051517150726
47997CB00001B/289